Letters From *Spirit*

Teachings From My Spirit Guides

MONICA TEURLINGS

BALBOA.PRESS
A DIVISION OF HAY HOUSE

Balboa Press books may be ordered through booksellers or by contacting:

Balboa Press
A Division of Hay House
1663 Liberty Drive
Bloomington, IN 47403
www.balboapress.com
844-682-1282

Print information available on the last page.

ISBN: 978-1-9822-6007-1 (sc)
ISBN: 978-1-9822-6006-4 (e)

Library of Congress Control Number: 2020924085

Balboa Press rev. date: 12/21/2020

Contents

||||||||||||||||||||||||||||||||||||||||||||||||||||||||||||||||||||||||||||||||||||||||||||||||||||

Preface

A day does not go by that I am not grateful for the journey I have been on. It has been filled with so many unexpected experiences at so many corners. The spirit world is very spontaneous and filled with beautiful gifts and surprises. It's one of the things I love so much about this road I have been on.

As I look back, I see now all the little breadcrumbs that spirit has dropped on my path to get me exactly where I am standing today. This is the same for you. We each are given so many breadcrumbs that are put on our trail to guide us where we each need to be. Do we see them? Are we looking? I was not always looking. As I think back now, I can see the enormous guidance placed on the trail they set in front of me—all the breadcrumbs so strategically placed in their perfect correct order at the exact right time. Some breadcrumbs I picked up, and others, I can see now, I stepped over. It is probably the same with you.

As I sit here and write this, I am overcome with emotions as I remember all that happened that got me here. This trail, this path, has not always been an easy one to travel on, but it has gotten me moving in the perfect direction where I needed to be going. This I am very certain of. Sometimes we walk down hard roads to get us where we need to be. Sometimes those experiences on our roads need us to look within ourselves. I had a hard time doing that on several parts of my trail. Why? Why was it so hard to see myself? Why did I not know myself better? How were there qualities within me that I was not able to see? Do you feel the same way about you?

Why were there breadcrumbs I stepped over? Were those breadcrumbs placed there asking something of me? I ask this question of myself. Is this a question you can ask of yourself?

My spirit guides—Edgar—helped me to uncover myself. They helped me to ask the questions and look within myself. Doing this helped me uncover qualities that were within me that wanted to be expressed and I was just unable to see. Edgar helped me dig deep, and then I made it a priority to myself to learn what my qualities were. This is how mediumship unfolded in me. This is how I was able to build this incredible relationship with my guides. This is how my channeling and working with Edgar became what it is now and what it is still to become. I am always in a state of becoming. You are always in a state of becoming as well.

My guides Edgar are a collective group of many who have been walking my path in life with me. It was so comforting to know this once I realized it. Edgar knew me more than I knew me. They understood me before I understood myself. They have known the qualities and potentials within me even if I didn't. They always have. You have guides also. You have guides who walk along your path in life also. I am not special this way. I am no different from you. We each have our own wonderful, loving helpers that give us guidance and put things on our trail. It is for us to pick it up or to step over it. It is for us to have the awareness of the guidance and the desires of wanting to move with the guidance shown us.

Edgar has been my greatest teachers for myself. As teachers, they have a great desire to teach and to help us. My guides are for me, but they are for you also. This is their desire. They want so much to help us all along on our journey here and make it fun, fill us with desires, allow us to understand the value for us to feel, to understand ourselves so we can know what gives us joy. They want us to know our qualities and ourselves. This gives us joy in our lives. Do you know? Do you know yourself and your qualities that lay within you?

The first book we wrote together, *"Destination Self – Navigated for You with Love from My Spirit Guides"*, is a short book designed to bring you closer to knowing who you really are and to help you live with more joy and purpose in your life.

This book, *Letters from Spirit*, is a collection of channeled letters given to us by my guides, Edgar, for each of us. Some were written through me and some spoken through me, but each were given with the intention to help move us forward. They were written with all of us in their hearts. In this book, through the letters, you will receive teachings from them—easy, practical, and modern teachings that you can read and feel into the words they express for you to nudge you along to get to know you more.

I am sharing with you in these next few pages ahead three channeled messages from Edgar to me personally. The first one is Session 1, titled "The Beginning of Much More." This was my very first voice-channeled communication. Up to that day, all of my communication had been through writing together. This process came spontaneously and very unexpectedly that day. As I always say, spirit is spontaneous.

The second communication was the next day. I was so taken aback by the previous days' experience and the miracle of this speaking through me that within me I had a great desire to try again and see what would happen. Therefore, I sat again with the intention to communicate in this special way, and once again, there they were, waiting for the opportunity, excited for the opportunity. This second voice communication is Session 2, titled "We Can Move Mountains."

These two communications are very personal for me and directly related to them, me, and our work together, but I want to share them with you so that you can understand how it all came to be and to give you a clear understanding of this journey I have had with them by my side and our work together.

My third session with Edgar, set the foundation for this very book as it was Edgar who wanted it to be written! You can read about it in Session 3 titled "Time to Teach".

Much happened shortly afterwards. One day I was fluffing the pillows on my sofa and received a clear message from Edgar: "Letters from Spirit on Facebook". I was compelled to sit and start receiving these channeled letters that are so uplifting and share them via weekly Facebook live sessions. This was their clever way of creating our second book together. The response was amazing. Edgar's messages really hit home for many of my followers.

I hope you also enjoy this book collection of letters from spirit, and my heart hopes you feel the love expressed for you through each teaching, as that is what is always intended …

With love,

Monica

Acknowledgments

There are a few people besides the publishers to thank for this book and getting it into the hands of those reading it today.

My guides, Edgar, must be first to thank because without them, this book would not be possible. They have been and continue to be my greatest teachers and cheerleaders, tirelessly working on me to see more of my own potential that sits within me. Working with them in this special collaboration is beyond anything I could have ever imagined. I say thank you every day. There is no love felt that is close to the same love that you feel from your guides, and I love them each right back.

I want to thank my incredible loving and supportive husband, Joe, who has been my solid rock. He has gone to all my live demonstrations and has helped me in any ways that I ever needed. He has always shown up and has been there for me. He has believed in me 100 percent, and his faith in me and support of my work has meant everything to me. He has been my greatest advisor, my ear when I needed to share, and at times a shoulder to cry on when I was too hard on myself. You are my everything, and I love you deeply.

My two handsome sons, Kyle and Cole, you are both grown men now, and I am so proud of you both. I smile as I see how you are showing up in the world. You both will always be my greatest gifts. Thank you from your mom's heart for all the love and support you have each shown me in your own beautiful ways. Thank you for cheering me on. I love you each to the moon and back, forever and always.

To my girlfriends who have stuck by my side through my transformation, through my long hours at work when I could not take your calls or return your texts timely, for the days I was too tired to keep our plans because of all my commuting between offices, for understanding that I couldn't share a drink because I had readings the next day, for respecting my need to stay clear, and especially for all of your love you have continued to show me. Thank you for being there for me. I love you all. I have been so lucky to have such loving friends who get me. What's a girl without her girlfriends? You are the best!

To my dad in heaven, thank you for teaching me such a strong work ethic. I learned from the best. I think of you daily. Thank you for your visits. I love you so much.

To my mother for showing me the value in being organized in life. I appreciate you and I love you.

To each of you reading this now and to those who joined my Facebook Live episodes, follow my social media pages, came to me for readings, and attended my events and/or workshops. Thank you from the bottom of my heart for being a part of my work that I am so deeply passionate about. You are all so important to me.

How It All Started—Session 1: The Beginning of Much More

This is nice, dear one, to sit and be here. It is what we want, and it is so nice for it to be what you want. You feel the change within you, yes?

Today is an opportunity for you to see and feel how this could be. We want very much for you to have joy in what you do. This is a time for you to feel and see if this is something you enjoy. So feel. How does it feel? How do you feel? You have made tremendous steps. This yet is another step. How does this step feel for you? How do you like it? Is this something you would enjoy? Ask. It is the beginning of more, of much more. And we are here to be with you, if it is what you wish.

You make us smile; to see you taking this time now makes us smile. To know the possibilities are endless. The degree of what you can do is endless. The levels of what we can achieve together are endless.

How does that feel? How does that feel?

There are many ways we can work, many areas where we can be together. It can be this, and it can be something else.

However, we wish to be with you. We wish for your light to shine brightly. We want you to be your potential. Do you? Do you wish this to be your potential? Ask.

We like that you have made this step, taken this opportunity, tried, for you can never know if you do not try. You never know your possibilities if you do not try. We like your fierceness. It serves you well.

Where shall we go from here? What do you want to achieve? What do you want to do? How do you want us to be with you? This is what we ask.

This is what you need to ask. You know. For you, it is just understanding; for you, it is just feeling; for you, it is just knowing what it could be. What it feels like and how you feel within it. So this is nice practice, yes?

We are not as different in voice as we are on paper. It is still the very same. We move slowly here for you to feel us, to feel the sensations we are providing you now, to allow you to feel whether this feels good for you or if this does not feel good to you. So we move slowly so you may know. All we ask is for you to feel. From the feeling, you will know, and from there, there will be more.

We have such great love for you. Your passion excites us. You are a special one. Know this: we have great love for you.

How It All Started—Session 2: We Can Move Mountains

It is nice that you wish to sit with us again. It is very nice indeed being together like this, sharing this time and this space, giving you an opportunity, again, to see how this feels, how this would be. You enjoy it, yes? It is important that you enjoy it. It is important that you find joy in the work that you do. We are happy you enjoy this.

From this can come very much. From this space and our being this way with you, and you being this way with us, we can offer very much—for you, for us, and for many. Isn't that nice? You see, being in this space offers much for many, offers much for you, offers much for us.

But first you must decide that this in fact is what you wish. As we said before, there are many ways to work, many ways to be together, many ways that you may shine your light. This is yet another one of them.

To say what can be, working together in this way, it is limitless. So much can come together from this place, this desire from you and this desire from us.

The most important is this desire we speak of—the desire that we have to be with you, to work with you. The desire you have within you to work with us creates great power, you see.

That power holds many possibilities, and those possibilities shall unfold naturally, organically, precisely. But first you must understand that this is yet another way of being, a wonderful way of being. For when you touch upon your desires, it is there that much is manifested, you see. Is your desire to work with us in this way?

Does your desire to be with us in this way give you happiness? To work like this, you must be happy, as there are many ways to be, many ways to work, many ways to discover ways of being together to bring our word out. Yes, the book is one; it is quite lovely, is it not?

This lovely book gives us much happiness. Does it you? We say it does. We are quite proud of you; it gives us much joy to see how it all comes together. [*Monica's note: Edgar is referring to our first book together titled "Destination Self".*]

Wait to see how it all is going to be, how it will evolve, how it shall touch others in the exact right way. Isn't that lovely?

You see, some will touch the book and enjoy the pages, every single one. Others will be drawn and moved toward certain pages, and this is fine. Some will be drawn to just the cover of the book, the image that it holds, the feeling that that image holds, and how it touches somebody.

They feel within that image—they feel the joy within that image—and they want more. Therefore, they read. And they find the pages within that hold that happy place for them, you see. It is different for everyone, and this is perfect, for you shall not touch everyone in the exact same way, nor should you.

These pages within this book will touch many in many different ways, for everyone's needs are different, yes? Everyone's heart is open at a different point, at a different place, at a different size. The openings are different, but we know that through this book, the opening within that heart will expand and will enlarge.

It shall touch and affect them in the right way that they are ready for at this time. And this is perfect. As we said, books are a beautiful way to express areas in which someone can look within themselves. As we speak now, this too is a perfect way to be able to receive messages that can open someone's heart. It is yet another way.

We may sit here and do it this way. We may write, and the words on the pages may affect somebody in the perfect way. The goal here, though, is to touch hearts, to affect souls in a positive way that moves people forward, you see. And you have this desire within you.

You have this ability within you to touch others, to move others, to allow others to see within themselves what their possibilities are. This is shining their light bright; this is allowing them to see that there is a light that is bright, which perhaps has just been dimmed.

The way we work together allows others to see that their lights are bright; it is just a question of finding that light. You are very good at this, you see. You are very good at inspiring, motivating, sharing. You are a giver; it is so.

You enjoy giving to others, and this is quite nice. We too are givers. And you and we together hold great power, for each of us holds the desire and the power to want to move others, you see.

We want to move others for their best potential, to find the greatness that lies within them; and yes, it is different for each, but there is greatness within everyone. So many do not see it. So many do not feel it. So many do not know it. And here we come to help show, to help guide, to help lead the way, for them to feel that power within them that stirs, to actually get things stirring, you see. To make people feel good about who they are, to allow that excitement within them to rumble, you see. Get things activated, you see.

It is quite well. It is quite good, this book we created, you and us together. Do you see the difference we can make for others when we work together? We know that this is something that you enjoy doing. We also know that this is something we enjoy doing. And together that power, that joy of wanting to do and be and create for us—for you and for others.

It is very powerful. Many shifts will happen because of this. People will find their voice, you see. People will start looking for their voice, you see. People who have been very quiet, uncertain of who they are, will now become more certain, you see. And this is quite lovely.

You are quite good at this. You are quite good at many things. But truly making people feel good about who they are, inspiring them to see what is within them, exciting them to look, to seek, so they can discover, is a gift you have. Moreover, it is a gift that we together can share to help others realize their very best potential.

Potential is a word we like to use, for when people can find their potential, when they can know their potential, when we can shine a light on their potential, they can make themselves their very best. *Your* very best is shining your light for all to see—awakening those who lay quiet, still, dull, who want to be active, who want to be bright, who want to move but do not know how … do not know where to move.

That ability lies within them. And then your light gets shined upon them. And then you show them. Together, you and we, we show them where it is, where that light is within them. But first we must show you the light that is within you, for it is quite bright, you see.

For you to be your potential, and we know you do want to do this, we know that your potential, to live your potential, to work your fullest, to be your fullest is of your greatest desire.

We know this. And we say you know this. Now it is just time. You are ready, you see. You are ready to be all that you are. You are ready to shine yourself and worry not about others. Worry not. Worry not of their path, worry not of their approach, worry not about their ability to choose to see your light or not to see your light. You have your own path, and your path is long, wide, and beautiful.

Stay on your path; worry not of anyone else's. You worry about yours only. You focus on yours only. For your path is going to lead you to much. *Your path leads to much.*

There is so much for you. Do you know why? It's because you want so much for others, you see. It is that intention that you set, each and every day, when you speak to people, when you meet people, when you read people.

When you think of others, you are always wishing for the potential of them, always wishing to make their light brighter, you see. This intention that you set, this energy that you set within yourself every day, is what brings the power to you, you see.

It is why we are here with you. We feel that energy. We know that power within you. We know your potential. We know your potential; we know who you are. And we know what you are here to do.

So let's begin. Let's continue. For you, there is always more, you see, always more that you can do.

It is wonderful.

We sit here and watch how you take on your life, how you tackle the things that we place upon you on your path, and you just go for it. You go, you do, you move with it. It is quite special.

You just go for it. There are no reservations. There is no limited feeling within you. As we said yesterday, *fierce* is a strong word. It is a meaningful word. It is a word that represents you—yes, it is so.

The way you go after your work, the way you go after wanting things, how you choose to want to go forward, trying new things, going after new things, even when you don't know exactly where it will lead you, you go anyway.

This is lovely, for you trust, and trust is a very important part of this work, you see. Trust is what is needed to carry out the potential that is within you.

Thank you. We say thank you for trusting us. Thank you for allowing us to be with you, for it is where our heart is. It is with you. Moreover, it is with the work and we know your heart is with us. And the heart within you is also for the work. Therefore, you see, you are not much different from us.

Together as a team, us doing what we need and you doing what you need, the force is quite great. Therefore, when we say potential, the two together, you and us together, collaborating as we do, we'll move mountains.

It is not necessary that you know everything. It is not necessary, for it is fun to just go along and see what discoveries present themselves to us. It is fun for you to walk along your path and discover things, new ideas, new ways of being, and new ways of working. Knowing it all is not fun.

To be and just allow and just go, this is fun. For when you approach work this way, it is always a journey of joy, and we wish this journey for you to be joyful.

We want much for your work to have happiness for you.

So, we ask, have you decided? Is this what you wish, adding this to the way we work together? How does this feel now? Quite normal, yes? Not so different, yes? Interesting too, yes?

It is important that you have interest, it is important that you are entertained, shall we say. Entertainment is what brings more inspiration for you, you see, through this entertainment and through this inspiration, it feeds more desires, you see. It is what keeps the fuel in the tank. So yes, it is important that you feel entertained in work. It is important that you find enjoyment in what you do, in your work, for that shall just give more and more.

And we will say that you are quite good. Every day you impress us. Every day you're warming hearts, you see. And this warms our hearts. You give so much joy to others through your readings, through your words, through your hugs, through your intentions of just wanting those with you to have an experience of love, to have an experience that is joyful, to have an experience that moves them in some way.

You are a helper too, just as we are. You are a giver, just as we are. You work from a place of love, just as we do. Therefore, as we said, you are not so different from us. Do you feel your power?

That unleashing of the power is so ready. Therefore, let us start. You, we shall say to you, look as we know this is so much in your thoughts, your new place of business, we say it is good to do. It actually will not be something that creates more work for you.

Instead, it shall create more happiness for you, you see. For this is the way that you will have more people to touch, more people to give experiences to. More people to shine your light on. And through shining your light, they find their light, you see.

You are expanding. It is so. Expanding is normal. It must happen, for it is not natural to not expand yet feel the desires and inspiration that sit within you, which seep out through you.

It is necessary to expand, you see. It is quite normal. It will all align—worry not. Keep searching. Keep looking. You will find your space. And it will feel perfect. From that perfect space that feels perfect, it will bring many. You will have many there, you will have many at your other office, and you will have many everywhere you travel.

People follow you because people want to go where the light is, you see. People want to be where the light is because light feels good. So many are in darkness, you see.

However, with you, they feel light. They see lightness, and they are attracted to that light. It is much like a firefly for you—buzzing around with your light showing, twinkling everywhere you go, catching people's attention through the corner of their eyes. It is hard to avoid, you see. You step into a space and you twinkle; you light up. People want that, you see.

That is why you are perfectly situated right as you are, because from the space where you are and the path that you are walking, it is not only shining your light, but that light is also leading the way for those, and from this place comes much happiness, you see.

When people can be with their light, connect with who they are, and brighten themselves up, they have more joy, you see. Therefore, you are creating so much happiness everywhere you twinkle, everywhere you step, because you illuminate. It is unavoidable. It is not that people cannot see it. It is not possible.

Not only do they see it within you because you have a glow; while this is so, they also *feel* it. And although you glow and it is beautiful to see, it is the feeling that people have when they are with your presence that truly makes them feel the light within themselves. And it makes them want more, you see.

Therefore, you will do great things. You will have great, large crowds. Many will follow you because you take people on a path, a path of happiness, a path of joy, a path of living their lives fuller, richer, brighter.

Moreover, we do this with you, through your mediumship, through your psychic sessions, through the speaking that you will do. It is so. Through your books, and we say there are more, more coming, more books, we like too for you to share your story, how your light was discovered, how you found the light within you.

You see, it is very empowering for others to see that this beautiful bright light that you are, walking your path and illuminating for all of those to follow you, was not always so bright either. From that moment, people can resonate with the fact that you too had a light that was dim, and how you found your light will inspire many, you see.

Therefore, there are many books, there are many conversations, and there is much to speak about. Your work is about brightness. You are ready. It is time. Come—allow it to occur.

We are here with you, enjoying every moment, watching every moment, feeling into every moment, feeling into every heart you touch. You see? That inspires us!

That creates more desire within us, and then, from that place, our power grows. So can you understand the power here, you and us together?

Us wanting to be inspired continuously, consistently wanting our desires to expand, consistently wanting to have the same for you, and you consistently wanting to have the same for others. You are an extension of us, you see. We are a perfect match. And know we know, and know we feel, the love you have for us. It is true.

We know how you love us. You too feel and know the love we have for you—and the love that you and the love that we both have for the work that we are doing, it shall grow quite big.

Do you feel the expansion of that light right now? Do you see? Do you see that the world we shine the light upon, we shall travel? You will go many places. Do you see that globe light up for you now, how it is illuminating? Those are your steps, walking in those areas, giving the light to those there.

So we know that you have decided. We feel your answer, we feel your love, and we know that you want very much to touch others, enhance the lives of others, to allow others to find themselves, their power, their joy, their potential, all their possibilities.

Therefore, we shall now begin. We shall move forward. Now we have that path, we know that road, and we know that you and we are aligned.

And you have committed to wanting to do this work. It shall go quick; be ready. People are going to find you in many ways. People are going to know of you from many ways, ways that you can understand and ways that you cannot. Word is spreading. Opportunities are coming. The world is being notified. Your light is being felt. We feel it.

Therefore, we leave now with an understanding of your heart, you with an understanding of ours. And we thank you. This is a special time, and we are so excited for the journey that we shall travel together and all the people we will touch and meet along the way.

We have great love for you always.

How It All Started—Session 3: Time to Teach

Good morning Edgar,

I sit to write with you. I ask for validation on my inspired thoughts, my thoughts on this book I have been feeling. I too wish to ask for guidance in my teaching. Is it my time to do so? Do I have the needed material within me to add value for those that come to learn? I want to teach if it is something that can inspire and help others.

Indeed, it is us here with you, as we always are. It is. We are your teachers, and we say we teach to help bring out the potentials and qualities of you, you see. It is that within you that very much has come to the surface and has grown. Once this happens, it takes on a beautiful growing garden, you see. We say that much within your garden is now ripe and ready to pick, you see.

Much time has been spent nurturing those seeds and growing your harvest, dear one. The flowers lay within you, this bouquet, but we say those trees are there as well. On the tree of knowledge, growing fruit is to be eaten and enjoyed. For what purpose is an apple tree if no one eats the apple, you see? It is funny we say "apple," as your book speaks of the forbidden apple. It is though we say your apples are quite healthy to eat and that it would be a shame not to share the apples with those who are hungry for them.

Do you agree? It is that those ready for the fruit will come. It is that the tree that is you is made to share. This means teaching, dear one. It is not that one should hold within them the quality you have and not share what has been taught to you. It is so.

We say that teaching is a fruit on your tree. It is a strong sturdy branch, you see. You must understand that we here are teachers, teachers for you. And then too, we are here to teach with you. The classroom is ready to open. Are you ready? We ask if you are ready to stand in the classroom and be a teacher. We say you are. We say to move forward and begin creating platforms of working in new ways. It is needed and necessary to begin, for your future growth, to step out and step in, we say. Trust that you will receive what is for you. The feelings of being inspired are indeed those apples on your tree wanting to be picked. Ripe and ready, you see. Allow the apples to be picked and nurture another through the apple of knowledge, you see.

You speak of writing, and yes, writing is a beautiful way to build upon teaching as well, is it not? It's a way for others to gain more, you see. We say yes to writing as well. We say be good, sit each day beginning soon, to allow us to come forward with the next needed topics to continue our book collaboration together. To add yet another volume to the collection of what we are wishing to have. Yes, a collection.

There is always an easy way to see the education placed on the pages. It's always easy to understand processes that will allow the readers to jump right into the ways in which we speak in the pages, you see. There is a simplistic way we wish the next book to be, you see. Guidance is always our focus. Upliftment is always the focus.

This new book we wish to collaborate with you will be a bit more in depth than the previous, as we now have gained a bit more traction within your world from our work together and our previous book. And now we continue, for there is a need. We wish always to be where there is a need to serve.

These books add great service to the reader. They are a beautiful way to touch another, a way for words to marinate within them, you see. Therefore, we say yes to a new book, another one is becoming. Sit with us as you did before. We ask for dedication, discipline, and time. We say to make this an intention for you to be with us for the writing; it will be a lovely collaboration once again. It gives us much joy to do this work with you, and we say thank you for allowing this to be, for it could not be without you wanting and allowing it to be so. We are excited for this time, and until we begin, we say there is great love for you.

It is so.

Edgar

Reduce Anxiety by Painting Better Thoughts

Good morning Edgar,

I am doing a Facebook Live on feeling anxious. Is there something you can express here that I can speak of on this topic that can be of help to those watching and listening?

I am excited to be here with you.

You ask for guidance on this topic of anxiety and feeling anxious, and it is so that many may feel this way. However, it is only a product of how they see themselves in the moment they are feeling it. That is all. It is how one sees or feels regarding themselves—feeling in control or feeling out of control, feeling empowered or not, feeling connected to oneself or not. You see, the feeling of anxiety is only a product of how they are seeing themselves and how they choose to see their situation. If people see themselves in situations that stir and linger toward the negative, it will produce feelings within to match that set feeling.

If people can see their situations as more positive, they can and will produce better internal feelings within, which then gives a better set feeling, yes. It is that all are in control of how and what they choose to see. It can be full, or it can be empty. Which feels better? Ask yourself what is it that one thinks. Is it that thought that gives those the feelings of being anxious? We can choose to think differently, but it takes the desire within oneself to want to do it differently.

It is the practice and reconditioning of how anyone feeling thinks. Is this situation that someone is in currently, which is what is making one feel anxious, truly the situation? Or is it how one sees the situation? We say it is always how one sees the situation. To begin painting better images in one's mind. To become the inner artist within oneself. To be able to see oneself as this magnificent artist. To know one has the paintbrush at all times. That it is the thought that creates the image. What am I thinking? What thoughts cause me to feel good and vibrant? What thoughts cause me to think thoughts of feeling unsafe or scared?

They are both choices of thoughts. Are they considering the power within, to decide at any given moment, to think thoughts that allow themselves as a painter to paint images that feel better for them?

It is simply a way to get one to understand that anxious feelings come from the choices each one has toward feeling better or not. When one can stop and recognize that protection is needed from one's own thoughts, this is where you will feel safe. That protection comes from having better thoughts for oneself. Is the glass full or empty? It is as simple as that, you see. Feeling more empowered. Knowing that how one feels is a choice in each person. It is a choice and a decision each one makes, whether they see it or not. It is nice to place a flashlight there.

The security they seek resides in the comfort of better thoughts, and those thoughts produce better outcomes. What are they painting in their minds? What visions are they walking through the day holding? What image are they stepping into? It can be very helpful for those to see themselves with the paintbrush and to know they can create any better image that will produce better feelings within them.

People feel out of control, when in fact they are always in control. They are always with the keys to their car. Are they trying to start the car with a bobby pin? We say, at times, they are. It is helpful to show them that they are always safe, that it is only their thoughts that make them feel unsafe. It is as easy as that.

Exercises to better thoughts can be simple and easy ways. I thought that. How did that feel? If not good, then practice a better thought. It is always them having the power to do it. What are we doing that gives us those thoughts? What is being watched? What is being discussed? What is being overheard? Each has the power to change the channel. They can always turn the dial to something else. It is much like the TV; many options to watch a variety of things—funny, sad, violent, inspiring. What are they watching? Is it a must that they watch or do they have the power to switch the dial? We say that they have the power to switch the dial. Do they? Hmm … This is their question to self.

Circumstances feel better once one feels better, so always lessening the anxious feeling is the way to feel better. It is there that the dial is changed, you see. It is there that new programs to watch and to listen to can come to their visual forefront. There are always choices one has, dear one, for those who feel there are none are truly not looking through the glass but rather at a solid brick wall. It is good to tell them this as well. You see, it is simple shifts that bring easy change. One must never focus on something being too big for oneself, for each has the power to overcome whatever they feel. It is so.

We hope this has helped you.

As for the writing and the book you speak of, it is coming, it is percolating, and the right time is soon. Now keep as you are doing, as you are moving, your beautiful stream of wellness as you are and know this stream has power, you see, with the intensity and force to move and go to great places and many, very many, will be touching the water of your stream, dear one. The beautiful healing energy of the water you are to your stream is a very good thing indeed.

It is so. Until next time, there is great love for you here.

Edgar

In this Time of More Time

Good morning Edgar,

Can you shine some light on us for what is going on currently and perhaps some hope for us all? Thank you.

It is a fine time for many here, and people see this as such a period of gloom. We say it need not be this way. It need not be that attention be spent toward the "what is wrong" instead of the "what is right" in this time, we say. There have been many wishing for time, more time to be home, more time to be quiet, more time to be doing things they have not allowed themselves time to do. More time to rest. To make time to heal emotional wounds. To be with family in ways that perhaps were not occurring. It is as though so many are turning against the very thing they have wished more of.

Ask and one shall receive, you see. It is that each have asked for, wishing for, more time. It is that through this asking for, it has become the gift that many now do not want. Does it need to be like this? No, we say it does not. It is an answer for so many who have wished, yet you fight to not use the gift that has been given. You choose to see it as disaster or destruction.

How is being with family, being with loved ones, and being able to have more time destruction and disaster? How are you seeing the gift that is given?

Again, we ask you to stay in the present. We ask you to enjoy the now. Not the later, you see. Too many thoughts have gone out toward the later, and we say it is time now to simply be in the now, you see. For when you each can reside in that space of being, you will find all you have been missing and lacking, you see.

21

You say the being apart or away from your normal routines is difficult. Is it possible, we ask you, that your normal routines were not filling you up? Is it possible that the constant running you have been doing is not of service to you? Each has asked in one way or another to receive, receive more time in the day to do what they wish to do, to play games with one's children, to sleep in a bit longer, to avoid the stress of commuting to destinations such as work. It is a time simply to be and to charge one's own inner battery. Many are finding the idea of being with oneself uncomfortable. However, many are now beginning to enjoy this. It is a decision within each of you to decide if you are to allow the pause button to lift you up or take you down. We say to lift you is always the intention.

Yes, there are sorrows during all great transformations. You have seen it in history books and even in several of your current lives here. It is through transforming that shifts can be, and a new blooming comes, you see. It is that your world is gathering the needed seeds to plant anew for you. A harvest of new ways of living and of being is coming.

Are you able to accept it? This is the very resistance many are feeling within each other and have felt throughout the world you live in. It is the resistance of change, but, dear ones, you must know that change is a must, for nothing stays the same. It cannot be. The expression of the world is shifting. You must decide how to step into this, for each of you are a part of the miracle of life and each of you must play a role toward how it shall transform you. Will it lift you up or will you allow change to take you down? You must each ask yourself this question.

When each can come to a place of acceptance and not resistance that things cannot be the same as they are, then the transformation can begin to bloom within each vein of every living thing. This includes you, dear one. It is a time of doom, or it is a time of growth. Which do you feel is better for stepping into life as it is becoming? It is always becoming for you, you see. It is always your choice. It is always your decision. It is always for you to decide how you wish to experience what is going on within you and around you. It is a time of decision. This is the pause button here now, which will allow you to ponder this, to spend time now and decide before life moves back with speed once again.

How fast do I wish to go in my day? How many stops in my day moving forward do I now wish to take to allow myself to smell the roses ... roses you each have planted for yourselves? They are there.

How quickly will you choose to race through your life once the pause button has lifted away? It is time to ponder and reflect on the miracle you are each blessed to be a part of and decide how you wish to experience this miracle.

We say to spend time here. Spend time pausing and reflecting on this a bit, and when life moves forward again to your different normal, it will be of your choosing now on how you want to experience it and with whom. It is a fine time. Whether you see this in this moment or not, we come together to share with you that all is well.

It is so. Until next time, there is great love for you here.

Edgar

Asking and Wanting to Become

Hi Edgar,

I sit today to write some more with you. I have no set topic. I ask if there is anything you wish to share for me or for others that I then can share.

Indeed, it is that always there can be topics and never a day there is nothing we cannot share or that you wish to ask. Asking is how all becomes, you see. It all must begin with the ask, the wanting to become, you see. It is that we are asking of you as well. To ask you to believe, to trust, to ponder, to enjoy. It is that we have asking, as you all do as well. You ask to receive. We ask in hopes to receive as well.

You see, what all do affects another. Each soul has a connectivity to one another, and therefore each one affects the other, you see. It is the community of life. You each live in it, grow from it, and expand with it. It is a wonderful time you each sit in. It is a perfect time to be, do you agree?

Some do not, you see, and it is there that a flashlight can be placed. It is a time to see the importance that you each have to one another, to your communities and to the community of the world in which you reside. There are many places in this world, yet no matter where you sit, you touch another; no matter where they sit, you see. It is that you each touch one another energetically. It is why all are now facing these times. If the shift within each can be placed in a new, better feeling direction, it too will affect all who sit in the world, no matter where they are.

All of you are placed within a world that is loved and protected by a greater world, a world of love—a world of compassion—and we wish more of this to be dribbled onto all of you in your world. Each of you can create a world of your choosing, a world with the experience of your choosing, yet you do not all play with the same book of rules.

It is a choice as well to play as you wish. There can be a thief, and the thief can steal and may steal more than once, but one day the thief will receive repercussions for the behavior of its own actions. We say that in several ways you are each the thief, the thief of stealing joy from yourself. Then stealing joy from each other by the treatment that is expressed by one another in your communities. It is a wish to have you each play the game of life with a better playbook, a more compassionate playbook for one another and for the organisms that create and sit within the world that give you the very life you steal each other away from.

We say to play differently.

Go about this beautiful life with compassion, with love. See yourself and others the same. Come together to be the oneness that you all are a part of. There is no division, you see, when you can see yourselves as one. We are one with you always. It is not that it could be any other way. The mere fight that is being fought to separate each other from ourselves separates each other from all that is. *Is* and *one* are two important words. It *is*, and we are *one*. It is so.

Begin looking out to all you see with clearer eyes, with more open hearts, and with trust from the deeper part of yourself to know that we are one. We are all connected, and what hurts one hurts another and then hurts all. All that loves as one loves another and then loves all as well.

It is a decision to be apart or to be together. An unwell feeling is felt within when you are not connected to the light source of all that is. We each are all that is, and it is a fine day indeed when all can begin dancing together and to love together to know that all is very well. You are each protected by the bigger light, you see, but it is that light within you too, and if all can brighten theirs, it will be a world of great dreams.

It is so. Until next time, there is great love for you here.

Edgar

Love

Hello Edgar,

What would you like to discuss?

Indeed, it is a good day to come together and be in this way. It gives us much joy to be here and to shine a flashlight on areas that we feel will be of help to you where you each sit. We spoke the other day about it not mattering where any of you sit, that energetically all can feel. It is the same here with us. We are excited for this opportunity to be with you all in this most wonderful way, we say.

Today it would be nice to touch upon the topic of love. Every person walking the very planet you reside on has love within them. It is true that some walk the streets not showing any love, yet you can see it pour out of others.

It is true that love is expressed in many ways and shows up in many forms. We are love, you see, and we show up here in a form unusual to many, yet we hope you energetically feel the love that is within us each as we speak these words to you.

Love may be expressed through gestures of touch, gestures of words, gestures of actions. Some of you live with your hearts on your sleeve, and others may bury that heart deeper within so no one can see it.

It is true as well that some walking your streets seem to have no love within them at all.

Through their gestures and activities, they may cause pain to others. We do understand that it's difficult to express love back toward one who seems to have no love within them, but we wish to say to you that there is love within each breathing soul that walks the world you live in.

27

How does one give love toward someone who shows none in return. It is tricky. Or is it?

When one who wears love on their sleeve or in their heart with an eager and willingness to share, a beautiful divine gift resides in them. It is a gift that all have but that not all have opened. We say to teach others to open their hearts so one can see and, better yet, feel the love within them. Therefore, they may know their gift. It is within all.

We say to be the light. To be the light means to shine your love out toward another. Can you find it within your imagination to see a beautiful loving light within you that is pouring out of you and onto another, imagining your light of love touching them energetically?

We say to help shine love to another, we say to set the intention each day to be a light of love, to be you. You are a light of love. For those who have felt love, given love, or have known love, you each can understand that it does exist.

We say to set the intent to share the loving light within you onto another. We say to begin making a daily practice of giving away love. You see, the divine gift of love that resides within you is not one that can ever empty. It is not so. By giving it away, it gives you more.

Funny, yes? Funny that you can give something away and yet more of the same returns to you? It is in fact truth, you see. We say there are many that walk the streets not ever opening the gift of love that resides within them. Once they have, there will be a shift within them. We ask you all to practice sharing your loving light so they may shift.

Be the flashlight. Place the love onto another especially if you can recognize in someone that they in fact have not yet opened their gift of love within. Be the one, we say, who helps them open the gift within. Helping another is helping a greater number, you see. One touches another. One's loving gesture touches another. It is an energetic flow that, once motion begins, will be a powerful stream of well-being. It is so.

We say that you are all loving beings, whether you understand this or not. You are each powerful in the ways you can positively affect and produce well-being in another. Do you know this about yourself? When love is shared and expressed and you can each place your loving flashlight directed toward another, you then begin to light them up with kindness and care—and then their hearts can begin to open.

This is the stream of well-being we say you can swim in. It is a way to lift each energetically to a higher place where all can feel and live within the love that has been intended for you all, no matter where you reside.

Are you each walking the streets with kindness and care toward others? Or are you each walking away from the one who displays the need of kindness the most? Ask yourself. Each must do their part. You say that in your world, 80 percent of the work is done by 20 percent of the people. We say to be the 20 percent. If you all can do this, we will have changed the curve and percentage entirely, you see.

Know that the one that shows no love indeed needs it most. We say to notice those and place your flashlight there so you can begin to make a rumble within them that begins to get them feeling differently. It is a wonderful thing to do, we say. We ask you all to be the love.

Set an intention of practicing compassion for the one who shows no love. Live from the heart. Live with the gift you have been given and begin to help others open the gift of love in their hearts as well. Love is to be expressed. We say this will create a beautiful world indeed.

We thank you for your time. We thank you for listening. We thank you for your hearts being wide open.

It is so. Until next time, there is great love for you here.

Edgar

Having Enthusiasm

Hi Edgar,

What shall the talking topic for our letter from spirit be today?

Indeed, it is a most wonderful time when we can be here in this way with you. We say it is wonderful to see you each gather as well for the letters we wish to share with you and for you. It is so, you see. We are here to shine our flashlight onto each of you, you see. We wish to shine our words upon you, and we hope it brightens you and lifts you each in the right perfect way. It is so.

We say that you each, in some way, find change a bit difficult. When things must be done differently, it gets you all in a bit of a ruffle, we say. We sit here and observe the very way you each step into your day. Some step in with bursts of enthusiasm and others with no enthusiasm at all. We say enthusiasm is the correct way to begin each day. We say enthusiasm is infectious. Would you agree?

When you see someone with such an emotion pouring out from him, it isn't that it does not touch you in some way. It is felt. Do you agree? When you see someone with enthusiasm, you ask yourself, "Where does that come from? How do I get some of what they have? I wish to feel that, yet I do not." Enthusiasm is a word that holds an exciting energy within when one has it.

Do you feel enthusiasm when your day begins? Do you roll out of the bed you awaken in rested and refreshed with the energy of enthusiasm? A few do, perhaps. Most do not. It is where we wish to place a flashlight.

Enthusiasm. What does it mean to you? What does it feel within you when you see someone expressing it? How do you feel they received the enthusiasm you see them expressing? Do you feel that there is a limited amount floating through the atmosphere and that that person was lucky enough to have caught it? It is so that you often behave this way.

Have you looked at someone who expresses enthusiasm and thought to yourself that you are going to have that also? *I am going to catch enthusiasm as well.* Can you understand that enthusiasm is about decisions to see your life for all it is and not for what it is not? So many see the life they live for the blessings they have not received rather than soaking within them the blessings they have received.

Enthusiasm is a mindset. It is so. Enthusiasm builds upon the way you choose to see something and appreciate something in your life. When you soak within the wellness of all that is right with a situation, it begins to form greater feelings within yourself.

Can you play more in your life, seeing yourself as one who is placed here to play? To play is to uncover, to enjoy, and to seek, you see. Are you stepping into your day playing, enjoying, and seeking? Do you roll out of bed with excitement for the play that is before you in your day? Or do you begin your day with an "I am grounded today" attitude? Are you playing or do you see yourself being grounded?

We say it will be difficult for you to find enthusiasm while feeling you are grounded. Many of you today feel grounded. You are not. You feel you cannot play. You can. Some of you have forgotten how. Where does it say anywhere that playing must be in a specific way or in a specific part of town or in a certain environment? Play comes from you deciding to play.

Can you sit at your tables in your homes and find things to play with? Can you find ways in one's kitchen to play? Is it possible to be in a bath and find that a way to play? Children do this. They look forward to a bath, bringing their toys to the tub, having bubbles. Many of your children wish to stay in the tub longer then you wish them to be in there! Why is this?

Can we learn from children? We say that indeed you can. Children can be the best to teach you to remember how to play. We say to remember that there were many times you each knew to do this. When was it that you forgot how to play? Ask yourself.

What began to transpire in your life when the play stopped and the enthusiasm left? Has it truly left or are you simply ignoring the very ways of living life that gave to you the enthusiasm to begin with? We say to begin playing, to begin finding enthusiasm within you once more. We assure you that it is all there. Everything you need to be joyful, happy, and content and living your fullest life is within you.

Is it possible you have perhaps looked outside of yourself for the things to give you joy? Is it possible that within you is where your joy resides? It is indeed truth to know that all one can ever need is within the very essence of you. You need not go to the market for it, or go on another vacation to have it, or meet a new person to experience it. It is all within yourself.

We say to become enthusiastic about waking up each morning. Seek things that keep a smile upon your face. When you seek, you then find it, every time. We say as well that when you seek to find things that keep enthusiasm away from you, you can find that as well. But why? Why decide to seek out things that steal enthusiasm from you rather than seeking ways to have it?

Both are available for you. It is you deciding every time what you wish to be seeking and what you find in the process. You are the shopper. You are shopping each day. You are walking with each step with an invisible shopping cart in front of you, pouring into it experiences that you are taking in from the day.

We say that the shelves are filled with everything you are seeking. What aisle are you walking down with your invisible shopping cart? Is it the aisle of enthusiasm or of gloom? Both are there for your choosing. What are you placing in your shopping cart? Ask yourself.

Ask yourself as well, "How have I been shopping? What aisles have I been keeping my attention on?" A grocery store has aisles of food not good for nutritional well-being and aisles that are very good for nutritional well-being. What aisle in life have you been shopping in and pouring experiences into your invisible cart?

We say that a mere redirection of your cart can take you to well-being. We say that emotional well-being is what we wish to highlight. It is a beautiful day here for us when we can see each of you shopping in the aisles and filling the carts with the things that give you joy. You then become the seeker of well-being and then enthusiasm will be in your cart. This indeed is a very good shopping day. Would you agree?

We say to ponder these ideas. Imagine yourself with a shopping cart and you are making your list and what is placed on that list becomes what you are seeking. Will you find well-being where you are focusing? Look at your list that is your feelings, your thoughts, and your actions. What aisle are you shopping in?

It is so. Until next time, there is great love for you here.

Edgar

Negative Thoughts

Hello Edgar,

Today's question for you: why do we have so many negative thoughts?

Indeed, it is again a delight to sit here and be with you. It is good way to give guidance upon your asking. We like the asking. When you ask, you receive, you see. We hope to be here in this way to guide you each to a better understanding of whatever topics you feel a need within to discuss. It is so.

You ask regarding thoughts, negative thoughts. We say that it is as simple as just that. Focus. Focus on anything brings it. When you focus upon the question of negative thoughts, then within you is the decision to play with it, you see.

Thoughts are a playground for you. It is a place of wondrous imagination. Many negative thoughts come from that imagination place, just as thoughts that are of a different direction do. We wish to share with you that your thoughts are you playing. Your mind is your playground.

Many of you are visiting the park all day and sitting upon the merry-go-round over and over and over, finding it difficult to get off. This is having more negative thoughts. We say that for each of you, your negative thoughts are much like a merry-go-round. Around and around you go until you become dizzy, we say, feeling a bit unwell from the ride you are on. The playground, your mind, has many places to play. Can you see?

There are many ways to use one's imagination. There are many ways to play and many types of rides to play on. We say to change the ride. Choose a different activity in the playground. Certainly, you each can know of other ways to utilize this playground, yes? The equipment gives the experience.

We say to try new equipment. There is more than just the merry-go-round at your park. You have a choice on where you give focus as you step within the playground to have experiences. When you go to a park, you stand on the grass. You look around and then you move toward an area in the park.

It may be the swings. It may be the slide. It may be a shady tree or a picnic table, you see. If you can all see that your thoughts are about your experiences, you will think about what you will experience. You experience through how you each feel. It is how thoughts occur for you. We ask you here how you are enjoying your playground? Do you decide which equipment would be pleasurable for you?

We say to spend time understanding how you like to play. Spend time understanding the experiences that bring joy to you. Is it a merry-go-round or is it a slide? Do you enjoy being within the experiences that give you pleasant thoughts or are you, out of habit, continuing to ride the merry-go-round? Do you see what we mean here for you?

Are you stepping into your imagination to play and onto your playground with the desire for a specific experience? Do you somehow want to feel dizzy and out of control, feeling as if you do not know how to get off the ride? This is you going to the playground and repeatedly choosing the merry-go-round every time.

Can you see the advantage to try the slide instead for your well-being? Try the experience of that equipment instead. Will it give you different feelings and emotions? We say that it will. We ask you why you always chose the merry-go-round. Thoughts that you hold are often ones that are repeated, you see.

Staying on the same equipment is you repeatedly playing the same way in your playground. Can you now see your mind as an amusement park, a place with so many possible experiences for you? When you go to an amusement park, are you only going on the merry-go-round? No, you are not. You are trying other rides.

Do you agree here? We say that an amusement park is much like your mind, creative and wanting to give you different experiences to try. Are you only going on certain rides when there is an entire park at your disposal? You have such variety within you to focus upon, so many rides to choose from. Yet many of you stay focused on the rides that give you experiences that make you uncomfortable, feeling uncertain and even frightened. It is so.

Imagine yourself in an amusement park. So many opportunities give you the desired experiences you want. Prior to entering the park, you know your intention is to have fun. You go to feel experiences that affect you positively.

It is not that you intentionally say you want to feel negatively, that you want negative thoughts and to have an uncomfortable experience. It is only that you are not willing to walk the park and play with all it has to offer you. You stay in the section of the park that offers only the merry-go-round or focus on the rides that make you very uncomfortable.

You are scared of heights and a bit claustrophobic, but you select a ride that places you in a small cage high in the sky and then falls toward the ground quickly with great speed. You feel sick afterward. Could you have enjoyed yourself more by having an experience on a ride that could have felt different? We say that yes, you could.

You can always decide what ride to participate in. You can always decide what you want more of or not. Negative thoughts are often repeated because you are not allowing yourself to think beyond them. You go again and again. You stay in that section of the park and do not venture further, you see.

There are many wonderful things to focus upon. Your mind is your park. You fill it with the type of experiences you want. This is your imagination. You are the one placing the particular rides within your own park. Can you see?

Can you see that the way to change your thoughts from negative to positive is to try another ride in a different section of your park? Your mind has great power to create any park of you desire. You are the designer of it, the builder of it, the cohabitant of it. It is all for you. When you can understand that your thoughts are a direct result of how you choose to play and what you play, what and how you design it to be, and with whom you take to the park is when the change occurs. It is as easy as this.

See your mind as a magnificent amusement park. In it is all there to give to you experiences. You are experiencing through the rides that are placed there. It is for you to choose which ride feels good to you. As the designer of your amusement park, you can have all roller coasters, all merry-go-rounds, or all water rides.

You choose. Your thoughts give you the experiences to have. You are creating your experiences with your thoughts, both positive and negative. Before stepping onto the roller coaster, ask yourself, "Is this the experience I am wanting today from my own personal amusement park? Your rides are your thoughts. Your experience will give you the feeling of fear or laughter.

What experience do you want? If you wish negative thoughts to decrease, then play on more rides that give you laughter, not the dizzy-in-the-head feeling. It is as simple as this. You are an imaginative soul with the gift within you to create your experience. Each ride you choose will give you an experience. Each thought will give you a feeling.

How does it feel? Ask yourself. Feel your way to better thoughts by playing on the equipment that feels better to you, you see. You are indeed a magnificent creator. If you want positive thoughts, simply create the amusement park in your mind and select the rides in it that bring you the joyful feel-well experiences that you wish to have.

It is so. Until next time, there is great love for you here.

Edgar

Be Curious

Good morning Edgar,

What shall we talk about today? I am always curious about what and where you like to place attention for us all.

Yes, it is indeed a wonderful day, is it not? We say it is. To be curious, as you say, is a wonderful thing to be. Would you agree? For when one is curious, there is an eagerness to uncover, we say. To be curious is a way to step into any day with a bit of excitement.

We also say that things that give you curiosity are also things you have interest in understanding. Would you agree? By being curious, you wish to understand more of something. This is correct, yes? Unfold the idea of something and play with new ideas and new ways of enjoying the play, we say.

We say to be more curious about yourself. Be more curious about your day. Be more curious about all that is around you. We say that there is not enough curiosity within you each being expressed on any given day. We wish to highlight this.

We see more of you doing it this way again. Going there again. Going in this direction again. Eating at that place again. We say that there is great value in being curious. It gets your inner engines moving toward more. This way of always doing things the same keeps you all a bit in Groundhog Day, correct?

It is difficult to be curious when you go about life each day the same way, you see. The same map. The same direction. The same routine. The same outcome. You land at the same place every time and with similar experience. Why?

We say that being curious allows you to seek, you see. Seek more of what is someplace else. Seek more of how you can be someplace else, you see. There is great joy found within you when you can step into a day with more curiosity, wanting to know more about something, anything, we say. It is through being curious that you each can begin expanding upon things that bring interest to you.

So many of you do not know what gives you interest. You stumble a bit when topics arise as to what shall we do today? Where shall we go? You have forgotten a bit here on how to be curious. Therefore, we primarily shine our flashlight here to get you to remember the words *curious* and *curiosity*.

What is it? What does it feel like to have it? Do you remember? Do you know what it feels like to be in a day feeling curious, being in an environment that gives you things to be curious about? Why do you travel? What is it about traveling that brings excitement to you?

You are excited for the idea of what it can be, you see. There is curiosity in the very idea of traveling. When you travel to places different from where you sit today, there is a curiosity within you regarding those places, yes, but also on how you will experience those places.

It builds curiosity within you, you see, when you can take your expression further then the "do it the same way every day" expression. We say to seek curiosity in your life. Seek curiosity in every day. It can be found everywhere. It is only that you are not looking around. You are limiting your visual output to be only within the areas of your own customized Groundhog Day. Can you see?

We say to step away a bit from routines and allow yourself to move with curiosity more. Seek conversations that build upon topics that you find curious. Prevent yourself from having conversations that are the same every day.

Do you find yourself doing this, holding conversations on the same topics? Ponder this and ask yourself if in fact you do. Be curious to speak of more topics, different topics. This is playing, you see. It is playing with words.

If it is not possible to go somewhere or to experience other areas within your city or community now, we say to begin with stretching the mind a bit more. Put into focus the areas of topics that get you buzzing a bit. This gives wonderful movement through you that then seeks to want more.

Can you see the difference here? Can you see how adding curiosity to your day will give you new fresh energy to move about? It is a better moving energy than when you stay in Groundhog Day, where everything is the same and nothing ever changes.

You go to the same places, eat at the same place, wear the same colors, talk about the same things. Can you see? It lowers your excitement radar. It is that curiosity within you that gets you wanting to feel new things and, by doing so, will give you new experiences to have, and by doing this, we say, will create new wonderful things you will find interest in.

With curiosity within you, you learn about what you like; with curiosity, you can find things and topics to be passionate about, you see. It is a way to express yourself more through your day, which will build upon the very foundation of excitement and joy, you see.

You are creative beings with a need to express yourselves, you see. Life is a beautiful way to express yourselves. Are you utilizing all that life has to offer you or are you staying within the small compounds of what you have allowed life to give you? Ask yourself.

Be one who thrives upon finding curiosity in things—in conversations, in people, in places, in situations—and watch that radar of joy soar. It is so. We thank you for this time, and we hope we got you all to feel a bit more curious.

It is so. Until next time, there is great love for you here.

Edgar

Past Pain or Trauma

Hello Edgar,

What would you like to share or discuss with us today?

Indeed, it is a good morning to be here with you and to share topics again that we feel can and will be helpful for those reading. There are many things we wish to discuss. We say that for today's letter session, we'd like to touch upon the topic of past pain or trauma.

The title says much. Past. It was and is not now. Many hang on to the very thing that has given them pain. Why? we ask. We say that experiences come in life in many ways, you see. It is that experiences are here to give you expression. To allow you to feel. To give you contrast between other experiences and expressions, you see. Many hold on to the experiences that have caused the deeper expression of sadness, pain, and hurt.

We say that when you take a vacation, you are experiencing and expressing *yes*. When you have a baby, you are experiencing and expressing *yes*. When having a baby, it is often quite painful, yes. There is in that moment and time tremendous feelings of pain and discomfort. When the baby arrives into the world through your beautiful gift of giving life to it, it is then over. The pain is gone. It is not to be felt any longer. You had an experience and gave expression during it.

When you go on vacation, you experience the location where you are. You take in and express yourself in the many ways you experience a vacation—the new streets you walk down, the different languages you may hear, the different scenery that you are now seeing that is different from your own. Yes, you enjoy the experience and express yourself through the experience. Once home again, you have a memory, yes, but you are no longer expressing yourself in that experience. You have collected experiences.

45

We say that with emotional trauma or with pain, it too is an experience, and through the experience, you express yourself.

When you have trauma, you often allow yourself to continue expressing yourself as though it is still occurring. You allow yourself to stay in the expression of that event or experience. You allow, you see. The word *allow* holds great power for you. It is you who allows, not anyone or anything that occurred that gave you pain to allow, you see.

When you have events in life that are painful, hurtful, or traumatic, you can express yourself through them while they are occurring. Can you see it as a script in a movie, with you as the actor? In the script, you are expressing the role of the character and then the film finishes and the movie ends. You were paid as the actor, and you then move on to another movie role that will again give you a different experience with new ways you can express yourself. Life gives you experiences so you may express yourself.

It is as simple as this, you see, if you can allow yourself to see it this way. The actor does not hang on to their previous character once the role they play finishes. The actor looks for new characters to play with and new experiences that they can express themselves through in a new role and in a new way. You are all in some ways the actors, you see, always having new experiences, new movie roles. You are the actors who express the character in the movie. Once the movie finishes, you are to move on to your next role.

Can you understand that these experiences that you have that are difficult, painful, or traumatic are movie roles that you play out as an actor? They are not meant to be played repeatedly. It is as a scene in a movie, you, the actor, expressing yourself through that role and bringing the experience alive.

We say to not hang on to one movie role. By doing this, you prevent other fantastic roles for you to play in life, you see. Do you understand what we try to say to you here? We say to not hang on to the experience in life that has given you pain and prevents you from experiencing other experiences.

You are not meant to relive the same role in life repeatedly. You see, this typecasts you. You are a creative being, wanting within you to have many expressions, many experiences that you can live life through. If you typecast yourself in your life, you will only get more similar roles, you see. If an actor plays mob characters repeatedly, he then becomes the actor all only know as the actor who plays mob characters, and the roles he is given will always reflect it.

Be the Academy Awards actor who is known to successfully play many brilliant roles in brilliant ways, bringing out many expressions of each character in its unique way that gives many experiences.

We say to live life, seeing life as this fantastic movie screen. You are the actor on the screen. You are the actor always wanting to play different roles that allow you to be creative and express yourself, gathering wonderful new experiences. Actors may at times play heavy emotional heartbreaking roles, it is so, but they may play happy, joyful, fun-loving roles as well. Do not typecast yourself in your life.

Do not stay within the pain and heartbreak or trauma of a past experience. It was a role in your movie, we say. Honor your work in it, the experiences you had from it and the gift you were given from playing it, for all experiences hold gifts. Always be looking for new roles that allow you to play differently. That allow you to express more and in different ways than the previous role, you see.

You always decide whether you take on a role or not. Nobody else may do that. If roles come up for you in your life that make you feel typecast, then we say to turn them down and move toward roles that feel better and allow you to express yourself differently.

Experiences you all face in life are there to do just that, we say—give you experiences. Just as with a movie you watch. If you do not like the movie, you can decide to walk out, turn it off, or change the dial, we say.

It is the same with your experiences that left you hurting. You can choose to press replay or instead you can turn the dial, you see. We say to turn the dial. You are in control of your emotional dial. No one but you has the controller in hand.

What are you replaying? Ask yourself this. Is it time to watch something else? Is it time to play a new role?

It is so. Until next time, there is great love for you here.

Edgar

Do You See Your Beauty?

Good morning Edgar,

I am here to sit and write with you. What conversation would you like to have today? What shall we discuss?

It is indeed a beautiful day, we say, whenever we are given an opportunity to be here in this way to shine our light onto you and those involved for these discussions. It is so. We say there is so much to find beauty in. Do you agree? So many beautiful things. So many beautiful places among the land you live.

We say it is also that each of you holds great beauty as well. Each of you has more beauty within you than any land you may walk along, you see. We say that many do not even place their focus here at all, you see.

We say that today we'd like to discuss "makeup." The makeup of the land, you see, is pure, natural, and always wanting to be just that, its own natural self. Its own natural beauty. Many of you do not wish this of yourselves. You do not all enjoy the beauty of your own unique individual, natural self. It is beautiful, you see. Each of you has some extraordinary quality that gives you your great beauty. It may be freckles on the nose of one's face. It may be the slightly crooked tooth that brings you great distress. It can be the beautiful heart within you that you are afraid to show.

You cover the freckles upon your nose. You bury upon your hearts dirt that prevents yourself from feeling. It is those feelings, you see, that give great beauty to you. Those freckles that are unique to your nose give great beauty to you. That crooked tooth makes you marvelously different from the next.

But you all wear makeup. You cover yourself from your beauty, thinking beauty must look a certain way. It is not so. Beauty, we say, resides in the uniqueness that makes one different from another. It is that there is no beauty to all being the same. There is no beauty in all looking the same or feeling the same.

There is beauty in the depths of your feelings. There is true beauty in the allowing of yourself to not wear the makeup that covers the beautiful freckles that lay upon your nose, you see.

Too many of you hide. You hide the beautiful qualities that are you. You hide the beautiful feelings you have that reside within you. You want to be this. You wish to look like that. You want to stand tall like the one you saw earlier. You look for beauty and see beauty in another but not within yourself. You see beauty in other areas but not where you stand.

You look and search for beauty in areas away from you, dear ones. We say that beauty sits within you all. It is like the beauty of the land. Your land. It is not that you must find it anywhere at all other than right where you are, you see. We wish to place a flashlight here.

We wish for you to look at yourself. Look deeply look at your beauty, your land, to find with your brilliant eyes the magnificence that is you. Take off the makeup, meaning the things you do that hide your true beauty.

If you wear makeup with the intention to cover the freckles, we say that there is no need. We say look at the beautiful markings that are especially unique to you. We say to feel within your heart what you feel, not to bury it. To know your feelings is a piece of your beauty. It is what creates the magnificence of you, dear one. That crooked tooth is a piece of you.

If all were the same, how dull it would be. If all places looked the same, how dull it would be. If all feelings were the exact same, how dull it would be. How dull it would be to have you all be the same, yet you fight through the days, many of you, to try to be what that one is and not what *the one* is, we say.

The one is you. You are the one to allow yourself to remove the makeup you apply to your life that keeps you from embracing you. To remove the makeup you pile onto your life to be what you are not meant to be, for you are all as you are intended, beautiful from every facet that you can see. If you could see yourself as we each see you, you would see the very magnificence that you are. There would be not any of you wanting or wishing to be anything other than exactly you.

We say you that have your very own brilliance. We say to embrace the brilliance placed on you and living deep within you. We say that there is makeup covering you, makeup of other people's expectations of you. There you find one layer of makeup. We see you looking to be like someone who is different from you, and we say that here is another application of makeup. There is no color more brilliant than yours is. It is the same for each of you, you see.

We say to see your own natural makeup. The one and only you. To know the layers of yourself without the makeup, we say. To understand that each layer within you holds tremendous beauty, we say. Tremendous beauty. Stop looking away from you and begin looking deeply within you. Wash away the makeup others place on you, which you have allowed, and begin to see yourself for who you are. Naturally beautiful from every corner.

We smile as we say these words to you, for it is a beautiful day when you each can see the beauty that you are and why you are perfectly created just as you are intended to be, with the love and with the glorious color, light, and flaws. You are indeed the perfect imperfect diamond.

It is so. Until next time, there is great love for you here.

Edgar

Staying Motivated

Good morning Edgar,

I ask to speak on the topic of motivation and the reason we lack it in our lives. Can you shine some light to help us be and stay motivated?

Ah, yes, a delightful topic. The word in itself fills up the being a bit in the area of motivation. We say words can be a very good thing to have when we speak of motivation. Words can motivate and demotivate. It is that within you, each has a scale, we say, and it is for you to understand what you place on each side of the internal scale.

Is one side heavier than the other is? We say that words carry weight—words spoken, expressed, and felt. When one says, "I do not feel motivated," it is in that instant that the body loses the filling of said motivation. Can you understand what we say?

To have motivation, one must first want it, you see. Then there shall be an expression from within you from what you want, you see. Motivation creates movement. Without movement, you may go nowhere, you see. Therefore, motivation is an important part of accomplishing anything.

From the organization of one's shelves and cabinets, to the growth of a business, to the enhancement of a relationship, all must have motivation to achieve. We say to begin with words that are lighter in feeling. Begin with words that are more frequently used in one's day, ones that can give you each the feeling of motivation. Why choose words that hold you in a place of not feeling motivation? It is what is done when one does not feel it, you see. Words spoken reflect the outcome of it.

All that you want to express must come from a feeling. If you wish to be motivated, you must ask yourself why. Why do you wish to be motivated? Why do you prefer being motivated than not motivated?

You see, the mere word *why* gets you closer to what you wish. Many make things very complicated for themselves. This is not a jigsaw puzzle with so many pieces to work through. It is far simpler, you see. Within your asking yourself *why* you wish to be motivated, therein lies a feeling within you, you see. Once the feeling is triggered, you then create movement in the internal body, you see. Now, when one truly sits with one's self with the question of why she wants it, then more feelings come.

We say that it is difficult to feel motivated when you do not know where you want to go. What are you motivated about? How can you get someplace with motivation if you do not know where you are going? It is keeping you driving in circles, you see. You cannot get there.

We say simply to ask yourself what you want. Ask yourself why you wish it to be. We then say from that moment of *why* and *want*, your engines ignite and now there is some movement within, just as when you start a car engine.

You cannot go without movement. We say that many feeling unmotivated simply just turned off the car engine. The car is there. The ability to drive it is within you. It is only that you have your engine off. We say to turn the ignition. We say you turn the ignition on by simply feeling into what and why. This turns your engine on, and by sitting longer now in this beautiful car vessel that we say is you, you then feel more, and here we say to turn up the imagination radar within yourself and play a bit.

This adds fuel to your vessel. To imagine not what you want or why you wish anymore, for your engines are now on. It is time now to imagine yourself driving there. How does this feel? How does the imagination of being in that expression feel?

You see, we say that motivation comes from desire. It is so. When you feel no motivation, it is clear that there is no desire toward anything. We say to find desire toward anything at all. Desire puts gas in the tank to ask your *what* and ask your *why*. Use your imagination to feel and even see the *what* and *why*, allowing it to give you an expression within you that feels good. This is what creates movement.

Know that you decide at every moment if you wish to be motivated toward something or not. If something you are doing gives you no motivation, then you ask, "What about what I am doing do I like, and why do I like it?" f you still feel no movement from the attempt to imagine from that space, we then say to move toward a different area of focus.

Motivation can be built upon. Begin wherever it is that gets the engines moving for yourself. Once the engine is on, the fuel through the desire of it filling you, you then can drive miles, you see. It can take you where you want and wish to be. See yourself as one who simply needs to turn the engine on. It is as simple as that.

It is so. Until next time, there is great love for you here.

Edgar

Remodeling Your Life

Good morning Edgar,

What topic have you selected for today's letters from spirit?

Indeed, it is a good day, for it is always a good day. It is that many days may appear to look and feel different from another, but all days indeed are good days. We say today that we wish to share the topic of construction.

We smile, as we feel you now a bit perplexed. It is that when you think of construction, you think perhaps of something changing form. Yes, indeed, it is correct. We wish to speak of construction and what it is and how you may see it in one's life.

You see, you drive down your streets and see buildings being created. You walk down streets and see spaces of businesses being reconfigured. You go down streets in which you live and see homes being remodeled. You see bridges being revamped and streets being repaved.

There is, we say, much construction all around you for the betterment and improvement of your homes, cities, and communities. Why the construction? Well, it is to make anew. It is to improve upon from the previous and to add on to so it can grow for the use of it.

You see that construction is all about in your world. You live in it every day. You are accepting of it as a part of how things go. Would you agree? It is common for you each to see it in your everyday lives. You walk past a construction site and think, *I wonder how long before it is finished. I wonder what this building will be or whom it shall service. I wonder how it will look once completed.*

There is a curiosity to you regarding much of your construction sites, we say. Would you agree here? We ask you if you have ever thought of yourself as a construction site, a place where much is being revamped, changed, updated. We say that you each are, in some ways, your own work in progress, your own unique construction site. However, do you ever look to yourself and wonder as you do at the construction site you see and ask yourself, "I wonder how I will be? I wonder how I will be of service. I wonder how this will all look."

We say that you pay more attention to the construction sites in your world than you do with the construction that is happening within you each. Do you understand that there is construction going on within you every day?

On sites, you see walls of buildings coming down, new walls forming. You see old floor plans being redesigned to allow more functional floor plans to meet the desire of the space. You see buildings adding stories and garages. Can you see that within you too is much growth and changes happening? You are indeed a beautiful construction site. Isn't that wonderful? It may feel messy, noisy, and a bit overwhelming to you at times, but this is how transformation occurs.

Know and understand that you have inner walls coming down within you, these walls perhaps being belief systems that no longer work for you, tearing down past events that left you unable to move ahead freely in life, and there is a need for new floor plans within you needing to be redesigned. Within you in your life, through experiences that you have, you grow, and from that growing you now need more floors, more rooms, more space to hold that expansion you have created from those experiences you have been given.

Isn't it wonderful to know that your landscape within you is always under construction, creating what is needed to be more of who you are? To make more space for more that you want. You each look at construction sites with this amazement and excitement of its completion and your wonderment of what is being created, but you do not look at yourself with the same wonderment of what is always being created within you, for you.

You have a beautiful design, an always-changing floor plan for your betterment. We wish for you to see yourself as a beautiful and creative construction site. A site within that always is changing and redesigning so it can stay current for your life and how you wish to express life in it.

In life, homes can look and feel outdated and need to be remodeled. Within your world, there are materials that change, and to be current, you must update and refresh your homes, with perhaps a new kitchen, new flooring, a need for larger closets. Many of you easily understand this, yet when it comes to updating the floors and kitchens within, you all get a bit uncomfortable. It is like walking on a construction site with no safety helmet upon your head and your being careful of each step taken.

Understand that change is necessary to your growth. To change and update your inner floor plan is necessary for your growth and happiness. We say to show up to your inner construction site with wonderment, just as you do when you see any new construction site in front of you.

Create those new floor plans, the bigger inner closets, and larger open spaces with far fewer walls, you see. Be excited for what is coming for you, for it will be beautiful.

It is so. Until next time, there is great love for you here.

Edgar

Navigating Uncertainty

Indeed, we are here together today in this most wonderful way, to be here and to help you each along a bit. It is that our eyes are focused much upon all that is occurring and happening in your world, in your lives, at this time.

We know and understand that it is a time of great uncertainty for many here, yet we see too that there are many who have managed to be more allowing of this uncertainty. We like this very much, for this allowing of this uncertainty that is among you is a very nice way to be. One can never know what is ahead, yes?

Therefore, in truth, isn't everything a bit uncertain? Yet many of you do not see it as that. But it is in fact truth that everything is uncertain, for there is truly no certainty in much of anything. And here we say that there is this wonderful thing we call trust. Trusting through the uncertainty is where you will find certainty.

We know and understand that many are wanting certainty, and it is the feeling of uncertainty that makes one feel unwell and uncomfortable. We understand. We agree that uncertainty can feel uncomfortable and that certainty feels far more comfortable. Yes.

However, we wish to speak a bit about how to navigate yourself through the waters of uncertainty. How to help you get through the day when you have no certainty. Not knowing what tomorrow brings. Not knowing what the afternoon brings. And we say that minute by minute, you often do not know what shall be lying before you, and uncertainty lies within each of you through your day. The big things that tend to come forward make the uncertainty uncomfortable for you all.

And what we say to you is that there is uncertainty in every aspect of your life, which is why the mere understanding of trust is important. What is it trust? Trust is allowing yourself to move ahead even when you don't know where you are going.

Trust is believing that an outcome will be there for you, even if you do not know what it is. Trust is allowing yourself, and we say the word *allow* because it is always within you whether you choose to trust or not. By trusting, you allow. You allow that you are bringing yourself toward more that is unknowing. When you do not know, you feel uncertain. When you know, you all feel more certain.

Why does it need to be that way? Why must you feel calmness only in the certainty of knowing? Why can you not find calmness in the uncertainty or in the unknowing? If you can, play here a little bit and understand that so much of life is giving you uncertainty every minute of every day. You do not know what you will be facing in ten minutes. You do not know what you shall be facing in five minutes. You don't know what beautiful thing will arise for you this afternoon or this evening, and how what arises this afternoon or this evening will affect you the next morning.

There is no real knowing.

We say that uncertainty is really how life is. There is no certainty, and we just wish to bring this to your forefront. To understand that it is okay not to know what is in front of you. That it is okay not to know how things are going to turn out. That there is this trust within you, that when you can feel and allow that in, it will navigate you through your day far easier.

You are standing where you are right now when you have gone through many things that have had uncertainty for you. In fact, there have been far more things you have navigated yourself through in this life of yours that have given you uncertainty than have given you certainty. Do you agree?

Navigating yourself through your life, so much has been filled with uncertainties. So much has been filled with the unknowing of what the next moment shall be for you. That is truly how life works. It is allowing you to go through life with the feeling of trust, unknowing what it shall be and just allowing it to be, you see. That is trust.

Can you do this? Can you be okay with the unknowing of what is in front of you? Can you be okay with the understanding that you are not to know what is necessarily in front of you? Can you move through your life this way? We say that you can.

But do you allow it? That is where your work lies, you see. For the things that come into play each day in your life, you are going to be unknowing of what those things are. Even when you plan things, do you agree that they change? Even when you feel you know something is going to be a certain way, have you seen it unfold differently? We say it does.

There is so much change and movement in life that is constantly moving through the energetic field in your life, and it is quite honestly impossible to be certain in any given moment or time because of the change that is constantly occurring within every movement of each person, the movement of everything that is among you.

The way others behave affects how you behave. Can you see? You may wake up one morning being quite certain in knowing and understanding that whatever is currently occurring that "this too shall pass." Then you speak to someone who has a different certainty, and that degree of certainty and lack of their certainty affects your feelings, you see. Within you, you will now create different energetic movement that creates different things to be, and this affects how you step into the next minute, the next moment, the next day, the next evening, you see.

Everything you step yourself into affects how you see yourself and your day in it. Each moment is constantly moving and flickering and changing about, we say. Therefore, it does not give you much value to know what is coming, what is happening, or what is to be, for it is always moving because there is no true knowing of what it shall be until it occurs.

However, there is a knowing within you of trusting and allowing it just to be as it is meant to be. And when you can step into your day with more trust, more of a feeling and understanding of your own energetic place, we say that things will be much easier for you.

It is so.

You tread among waters now that are quite rough. However, we come to say to you that there are patches within this water that are quite smooth. If you can, see this moment in time as a body of water, an ocean and currents moving through it, some currents stronger than others but the currents taking you where you need to be.

This body of water—being your life and you—is being a boat in that current of water. See yourself as a boat traveling on the water, the water being your body of life as you see it, and yes, some currents are rough and some are uneasy in feeling. But you also know through life this boat that is you.

You have traveled through many currents, and those currents have also given you new directions for life and taken you to wonderful places. While traveling through those currents, you did not always understand or know where they would lead you, but they brought you somewhere, did they not?

This is no different. Just understand that the currents of life in this moment may feel a bit stormy and there is no compass in hand to understand your direction of where the currents are taking you, but if you can sit within you and feel into your trust, you will know that you have been through many currents before.

You have been that boat traveling on rough waters and through currents before, and you have always found land. Therefore, you are simply in a time of travel now, you see. Where the travel will take you, you do not know. And we say that you do not need to. Accept the journey that you are on and understand that the journey will take you exactly where you need to be.

You do not know where it shall be, how it shall end up, where you shall find land, and what that land shall look like, but you are traveling through life now being directed by the currents to new territory. New land. Be good with the understanding and keeping trust by allowing yourself to know that it shall all be fine. Understand that that place will hold great beauty for you. Can you trust that? Can you?

Can you trust that although the waters are a bit stormy and sometimes the sea in which you are traveling on may make you feel a bit ill, uncomfortable, even seasick. We say to know that there is purpose in this journey and that this journey will lead you to a new destination again, bringing you to new land again? It always has. And it will again.

We say for you to just stay focused only on trust, to focus only on how you feel when you trust, you see. You cannot feel certain in times like this. It is so. However, you can feel better when you have trust. Therefore, we say to put focus in your trust so you will feel better. And move to the past a bit here, we say, to build upon the trust you need now, simply by looking behind you and understanding that the boat you travelled down on in the past has led you down waters before and those waters have taken you through different storms—some rougher than others but indeed storms.

However, the storms subside, and you know this. You know that weather conditions do not stay the same all the time. Storms move in and move out. We say for you to remember that as you build upon your trust within you and to keep your certainty there instead.

Allow yourself to be brought back to places that gave you experiences that led you to the knowing and understanding that the storms pass. Look within you. Look in your past. Where have you been the boat traveling down the ocean waters and taken down currents that felt uncomfortable, that felt uncertain, and yet it brought you to land again—land that was better?

We say that there you can find your trust. There you can find the knowing and the trust that all will be quite well. Belief is a very important, powerful feeling, for when you believe, it holds within you a comfort, we say. We ask you what you are believing? Are you believing that these uncertain waters are taking you nowhere good or are you believing that these uncertain waters are taking you somewhere wonderful? What are you believing?

These waters that you are traveling down now feel rough at times, but can you believe that the water then calms, that the currents calm also and the sailing then becomes far easier and far more enjoyable?

If you look into the past and into those journeys you have experienced already, you can recognize that they have brought you to places and filled your being with confidence and strength within you, giving you a new direction to focus upon to do things in new and exciting ways. If you can, you will then see that those journeys have taken you further in life.

We say to allow yourself to believe and to trust. Moreover, it is helpful to look at your past and to remember those waters that you have traveled through before and to know that it has gotten you somewhere and always guided you back to land. Although waters that felt rough and once murky-looking had indeed cleared and calmed once again. We say that this is no different and trust in that.

We hope this gives you something to ponder, somewhere to put your focus. Uncertainty does not have to be an uneasy feeling. It is only your believing that uncertainty should give you an uneasy feeling that makes you feel so, and if you can change the way you believe the purpose of what uncertainty in your life is, we say that it will begin to make your waters calmer.

And this, we say, will be very nice, for it will allow you to enjoy this journey with more of an adventure mentality within you as opposed to one that gives you fear. Even though some adventures may have moments of fear when you are experiencing them, the fear does feel different, doesn't it, when you see it as an adventure? There is more of an excitement to the fear, and we say to look upon it that way as well.

Your world is always filled with adventure, you see, and some adventures take you to further places, but some adventures come with some struggles as well. Therefore, we say to look upon the struggles that you may be feeling; your trust and belief will help you navigate through those struggles.

Can you look in your past and find that there were some adventures for you that also had some struggles and perhaps some of those struggles placed you in murky waters? However, the currents eventually took you somewhere that made you better for the struggles. We say that it has indeed. We say that this is no different.

Therefore, we say to trust.

Sit with yourself now. Close your eyes. Remember a time when you were traveling on that body of water, you being the boat. And think about the times and feel into the times where some of the currents were rough and some of the currents less rough. And on that journey, you being that boat, you traveled on that body of water, traveling through currents that felt uncomfortable and uneasy, and you could not see land anywhere.

There was no land to be seen to travel toward; there were only rough waters surrounding you. All you saw were struggles. All you felt were the currents below you taking you somewhere unknown and you had some fear but then realized the water was simply moving you to where you needed to be. And the water became calmer. The feeling of the rough water was no longer present beneath you.

As you looked out, you no longer saw rough waters surrounding you; instead, you saw land and then knew where you were going. You were navigated toward something else and somewhere else, you see. You found your new land.

You are being navigated somewhere again, and it is for you, as the boat, to decide, as you make your way to that new land, how you will step off of the boat, how you will step onto the new land changed. How does that feel?

Ponder this and know that whenever you feel you are on a body of water that is rough and uncertain, land surrounds you—and you will get to that new land. That land will be for you to design. Therefore, while on this boat now, traveling on these waters that feel uncertain, think about how you will be designing it when you arrive to the land. How will the land look for you? How do you wish to live life when you get there?

We say to put focus there.

We are happy to be here this way for you, giving you things to ponder, new ways of seeing things, and we hope this has been helpful for you all.

It is so. Until next time, there is great love for you here.

Edgar

The Light within You

How does one find that light within?

The light is found by wishing to discover it, by first recognizing that it exists inside. One must feel there is a light within them. That is the first step. Knowing that there is a light that may shine, we say that is the first step to understanding all that they are.

So how does one do this? How does one recognize that in fact they have a light? There must be a knowing within them. When somebody feels well and then they do not feel well. When someone is feeling joyful and then not joyful. That contrast of emotions is what tells you that there is a light and then the light was turned off, you see.

The joy is what illuminates the light. That joyful feeling is that light on within, and that feeling of sadness, anger, hostility, or depression is showing that that light is turned off. Therefore, to know that you have a light is knowing in a moment how you are feeling.

Those feelings are a direct connection to that light. That light is a very deep part of someone. And to feel in a place of happiness, gratefulness, joyfulness, contentment, or excitement, those feelings are connecting you to that light, you see. When we have pain, suffering, hopelessness, depression, sadness, anger, and hostility, these feelings notify you that that light within is off.

It is not so much truly understanding "Do I have a light?" as it is more understanding whether your light is turned on or whether it's turned off. Is my light shining or is my light dim? The way we know this is by the way we interact through our day. How we feel through our day. How we express ourselves and think of ourselves through any given day.

You may have a day where your light is on and another day your light is off, a day your light is shining brighter and a day your light is not shining at all. You see, that light is within your feelings. Those feelings communicate to you where and if your light is being shined.

Therefore, to know we have a light is knowing that we exist. The light is who you are. It is the existence of your very being. It is how the light wishes to be expressed; it is where we wish to place focus and attention. Where does your light shine itself best? And is it shining itself at its brightest? What degree of light is shining?

You will know by how you feel. You will know how your light is shining by how you feel. Ask yourself, "How do I feel?" How do you feel in any given moment? How do you feel at any given time? How does each situation that you step into make you feel?

You may shine your light in a hundred different ways each day. What things make you shine your light bright and what things dim your light? These are things to pay attention to, we say.

Happiness is found when our lights are shining brightly. When your light is shining at its fullest is when you live life at your fullest. It is that easy, yet so many lights are dimmed, people going through their days struggling, hurting, living in confusion, living with the discomfort of uncertainty. That is a light dimmer for sure.

When you have uncertainty, you have no power. When we feel no power, we have nothing to raise the dimmed light. That light needs power. That power is your source of energy. Your power is your energy source. It is your electricity box, that utility box with the electricity that directs the power to you, yet there are so many people experiencing power outages, it seems.

These frequent power outages within one's soul are what get you walking in the darkness without the light shining on you, within you, and upon the things in their day. People forget how to turn that light on, and we say to you here that that energy source is your power. It is your power box. You must stay in your power. You must know your worth.

You must know your power.

Worth and power are truly the same. When someone feels worthless, there is no power. When someone feels worthy, she has power. So how you step into the day, how you feel about who you are, and how you tackle the things in your day will always reveal whether your power box is on or not. Is there power going to you? How do we know?

You must ask yourselves these questions. You must always know and pay attention to how you are feeling throughout your days. When circumstances arise, just stop, pause, sit back, watch, and listen to what just occurred, asking yourself, "How am I feeling about this? How is this making me feel? Am I feeling empowered or disempowered? Am I turned on or am I turned off? Am I walking with lightness or am I walking with darkness?"

Your emotions will always tell you exactly how you are. Do you understand? When you are feeling joy and happiness, you are walking in lightness. You are connected with the power source that is you. This is so.

See that you are the source of your own energy and that your energy is controlled by your own circuit breaker and that your circuit breaker is manipulated by the emotions that you each attach to things and the experiences of your day. It is truly that. That is where the light is. The light is within you.

It is you knowing what controls the power source. It is how you step into your day, how you respond to your circumstances, how you engage and interact, how you feel within those interactions, and how you react to those feelings at any moment that controls the degree of light expressed.

In time, when you don't pay attention to your power source and don't pay attention to your light and whether it is on or off, you may begin to go through your day having feelings that do not feel good, not having feelings that are uplifting for you, and you don't feel empowered or connected to yourself.

You don't feel joy, and you don't feel desire or purpose. You see, when you are detached from all of these things, this is you not being connected to your power source. Your circuit breaker has been shut off.

When you are in your home and you realize an outlet is not working, you cannot get electricity from that outlet. You try to plug in your radio, your phone charger, or any device that needs electricity and it is not working.

You go to your refrigerator door and it is now dark, with no coldness coming from it. It is not connected to its power source. Therefore, you go to the hallway or utility room and flip the switch on the power box. Bingo! You have power again.

That flipping of the switch is you, all of you, making a decision to change the way you choose to see that circumstance in your day. That switching of the switch is you seeing and deciding to go about it differently. It's about paying attention to how you feel and recognizing that something does not feel well to you. When you open that refrigerator door and see that the refrigerator has gone dark and is not as cold as it should be, you know that the refrigerator is not connected to its energy source. It is not connected to the power source it needs to work properly.

So many of you walk through the day disconnected from your power source that allows you to live as you were intended to. We say *enough!* Do not be that refrigerator not connected to the energy source and letting all the food become spoiled. Don't be disconnected from your power source that keeps you from your full potential.

The refrigerator is meant to run efficiently. Its potential is to run cool and at a specific temperature in order not to let the food spoil. You all spend your day a bit like this refrigerator—not connected to your power source that is you. Being disconnected to who you are disconnects you from the power source; you stop running efficiently, and your light is no longer bright or cool, like the refrigerator not working properly. In time, the food spoils.

Those are your feelings. Being disconnected is what causes bad thoughts, bad feelings, and emotions through the day and then the next day, having these feelings of disempowerment and feelings of not being worthy. This continues when you are not connected and are having feelings of not being enough. Not being pretty enough, smart enough, sharp enough, ambitious enough, loved enough.

The list goes on and on and on. When you are connected and running properly, you feel better. You feel worthy. You feel loved. You feel beautiful and accomplished. You feel ambitious, lively, and inspired. You are connected to that energy and to that power source.

The goal here is to realize that when you are disconnected from that source and when you are connected to that power source, you see. It is a very powerful source of energy and far more powerful than that refrigerator. It is much more powerful than that electricity that the refrigerator needs to be connected to.

Your power source is far stronger than that. It holds much greater power than that refrigerator, yet many do not choose to connect to it. You go day in and day out, day after day, unaware that you are not connected, unaware of that power source not working, that the line has been cut and the connection lost.

You are going through the day not having good experiences; you don't feel well about yourself, with not enough joy in the day, and tomorrow is more of the same. These feelings build within you and this, we say, is the food spoiling.

Do you wish to be a smelly piece of fish? Do you wish to be a carton of milk that has soured? Do you wish to be a block of cheese that has become inedible? Do you choose to be a box of ice cream that has melted? Ice cream is not made to be eaten melted. Milk is not to be drunk spoiled. Some cheese should be moldy, but never inedible!

Yet many go through their days similarly, living with experiences that do not give the happy feelings and joyful way of being, walking through the day like a carton of spoiled milk, and you wonder why you do not feel right. Why does your tummy hurt? Why you don't feel well? What do you do? You take pills; you medicate. You stay in bed.

You begin to accept life as a degree of unexciting circumstances, and many have simply accepted life to be this way and have gotten quite used to walking through the days in darkness with a dimmed light. We say it is time to begin doing it differently. It is time to get that energy moving through your body again. To plug in. To connect.

How do you do that? Be with yourself. That light is within you. That power source is you, you connecting with that source energy, that light that is wanting to be so bright. All it needs is for you to decide to go about your day differently. Isn't that interesting? All that is needed is a decision—to decide to live happier will create the very thing that turns the light back on within you. It is no different from flipping the switch. It is a decision.

You open the refrigerator and see it is not working. The light is out. You recognize the temperature is no longer cool as it should be. You know something is not right. The refrigerator is not working. What can I do? So, you go to the breaker box and flip the switch; you then go back to the refrigerator and open the door and you see that the light is now back on. Ah, the connection is back. My food will not spoil. Phew. Thank goodness.

There is no difference here now with each of you, really. There is *no* difference. Be aware if you do not feel good, if you do not feel right, if you feel off and not in sync to what feels good. Choose to feel different. Flip the switch.

Ask yourself the following questions: What does not make me feel well? I shall not do that again. Who do I spend time with who does not make me feel good about myself? Choose not to spend time with them. What is it that makes you feel disconnected? Ask yourself. Stop and recognize it, just as you opened the refrigerator door and saw that the light was not on and the temperature wasn't cool.

As you step into your day and you experience something that does not feel good to you, making you feel off and not right within, stop and open that door to self. Ask yourself, "Why am I not feeling right? Why does this not feel good? What experience have I just had that made me feel this way? What made me feel sour? Be made aware and choose to do it differently. That is switching the switch.

If you can go through the day always checking in and being sure your power source is on and working, you will know, just as when you opened the refrigerator door, that the light is on and the temperature is cold. You will also know by how you feel, each time you step into your day, how it should be. Simply try. We say to make this a lovely exercise. We shall name it "the refrigerator door exercise." It is fun. It is important to have fun. Connecting with your soul should be fun. Connecting to all that you are and the power within you should be fun.

Therefore, we leave you here to think of this, of yourself, as a tremendous power source. This is your light. It is very bright and very powerful, and it can be a source of energy for many things. Your job is to be sure that it is always turned on, and that you are always connected to it. Go play with this exercise. Connect with yourself and the light that sits within you and know that you are very well, very powerful, and that you can do many things and do them greatly.

That is all for now. We thank you for this time and being in this way with you.

It is so. Until next time, there is great love for you here.

Edgar

Finding Confidence

Good morning Edgar,

I wish to sit with you today and speak about confidence. What is it? How does one get it and how does one hold on to it?

Good day to you. It is a fine time as we sit here and come together to speak of a subject of your asking. *Confidence.* We say that it is a good topic to touch upon, for we see many struggles with this way of being. We say *being* because confidence is within your being. When one has confidence, they have touched the very being that is them.

When one feels confident, they are directly connected to who they are, you see. It is only when one feels not confident with themselves that they are simply not tuned into their very own frequency. We say "frequency" here as it relates to each one's energy system. It's all energy, but how it moves and takes form is different to each, you see.

When you are connected to yourself, there is an energy of confidence. Confidence is energy moving through you, and not being confident is also energy moving through you, you see. How does one feel when confident? Well, you feel vibrant, certain of self. When you move forward with decisions, there is an energy toward that as well when you are confident or not. Do you agree? We say that it is important to understand that confidence is an energy that is in you.

This is why we say that being confident is being connected to self, for all you need is within one's own being, you see. Therefore, we say that becoming confident is knowing yourself. We have stated many times in many ways the importance of self, and here it becomes important to mention it yet again.

When one feels assured of their direction, they feel confident. When one feels positive with one's decision they have made for themselves, they are confident. When one moves toward an area in life where they have not gone before and yet they go anyway, there is confidence, you see. When someone believes in what they are doing, whether another agrees or not and they do it anyway, there, you see, you find confidence.

It is all energy toward how one is living. To live in confidence is living with the light on within you, shining bright and unaffected as to whether that light is too bright for another. When you are confident, you shine your light in its fullness, you see. We say that not all like a bright light, and we say that it is not for another ever to dim your own light when someone decides not to like its brightness.

It is the same here in confidence, as we say that many second-guess their actions, their decisions, their direction, their purpose, all because that light shining confidence in these areas is too bright for another to be comfortable with, and then they react from this energy, and we say that this is a marvelous way to dim the light.

Where there is no light, there cannot be confidence. Confidence needs the energy of the light, you see. When one feels confident, a source of energy within them takes them to great places, yet opinions prevent so many from venturing to those places. Why is this? Why is that such a problem?

Acceptance. We say that many need acceptance. Why? Looking away from themselves and looking to another for acceptance keeps one away from their confidence. You see, dear one, confidence is an internal job, not one that can be shared with another. What we mean by this is that your confidence cannot come from another. Many confuse confidence with validation.

These are two different things. Being confident is standing firmly on the ground with an inner knowing of who you are. Validation is wanting others to see and agree that you are standing firmly on the ground. Do you see?

One cannot create for another inner confidence. That is an inside job, we say, so do not confuse confidence with validation. They are completely different energies and should never be blended together. When you wish for validation from another person, group, family member, colleague, or organization, for instance, you are looking to be seen for what you feel within. This is validation, to be noticed for your efforts made moving toward what you feel within you and where your decisions and directions are placed. Why? Why do you need this? It is a personal experience to feel confident, we say. It is something only each can feel individually, so many confuse it with the energy of validation.

When one does not receive the validation that one is seeking, it dims the light of confidence. Therefore, we say to keep your confidence personal. We say to know and understand that confidence is given to you only by you; however, it can be stolen by many. It cannot come from another source. It is your own relationship with yourself toward what you are doing, how you are doing it, and the road you are traveling down to do it, you see.

We say that confidence lies within you knowing you. We say that confidence is a relationship with you and what you believe about what you are doing, how you are doing it, and where you shall do it. Once you request others to join in here, energy then changes. We say not to confuse confidence with validation. To ask for validation is inviting others to enter your own relationship with your confidence.

You must understand that. Validation and the need for it will always make your confidence less, for whenever you seek outside of yourself for what can only be found inside, it never feels quite right. Doubt surfaces and you then begin to change the very energy of your confidence as well. Can you see? The light dims more.

You ask how one keeps the confidence once it is felt. We first say bravo to having it. Having confidence in self and with what self wishes to express is perfect. To have this, and in addition to move in the direction of what gave you confidence, we say that is always the path for you, you see. It cannot be otherwise.

We say that to keep the confidence is to stay always within the feeling of your own relationship with it. It is yours to keep, you see, until you choose to give it away to the need for it to be validated. Keeping confidence means not wishing validation. It is as simple as this.

Understand that confidence is an inner job that requires no one else but you. It is so. We say that we love the questions and hope we gave you something that will help you always know your confidence of who you are, why you are as you are, and to never step out or away from what feels good. We say that needing validation does not feel good, so we say to stop moving in that direction of energy, as its energy is quite different from confidence.

It is so. Until next time, there is great love for you here.

Edgar

Letting Go of What
No Longer Serves You

Indeed, it is nice to sit with us and make this time to work together in this way, for there is so much work that lies ahead for us. And we say that it is an exciting time to be here and work in this way. You will see that it will give great value, so to speak, concerning a topic for our teaching topic.

It is a time of reorganizing, you see. Your life there as you are is indeed a time of spring-cleaning, as many of you say. And it is so. When you look upon your homes and you look at your garages and your closets, there comes a need to reorganize them, clear them out. Go through what you have stored within your closets, your garages, and your drawers.

Many drawers need reorganizing as well. Would you agree? We say that this time of reorganizing gives a good opportunity for you to see what you have been hanging on to in your closets, your drawers, your garages. When we speak of your drawers, your closets, and your garages, we mean you.

What have you been hanging on to? What have you been holding on to and not wanting to let go of or give up, thinking there may be a need to have that? We wish to say that there will never be a need to have those things that you hang on to. We say that this time of reorganizing is an opportunity for you each to look within the drawers that are within you.

Look at your inner closets that are you and begin to go through what you have been storing. We say to take each item out, look at it, and ask yourself, "Has hanging on to this, has storing this deep in my closets, given me any value? Did I even know it was within me?" Sometimes there are things stored deep within your closets, and in those closets deep within, you find things you didn't know you had been storing.

As you pull out an item and focus upon it, you remember the purpose of it, and here is your opportunity to look at it again and feel and ask yourself, "Is there indeed a need for this any longer? Does this still serve me for who I am now? This is something I have been carrying around, kept, and stored for so many years that I forgot it was there.

If you can see yourself as a bit like a closet that hangs on and stores things, not wanting to let go or give it up or give it away, we say that many things in your closet can be given away. Will you allow yourself to do that? Will you allow yourself to give away what is deep within your closets?

As you go through the drawer in your kitchen, you have this miscellaneous drawer where you store random items. In the beginning, that drawer is not so full. That drawer serves a good purpose to hang on to items you do not know where to place, so you title this drawer the junk drawer, the everything drawer, or the miscellaneous drawer, storing things in it that do not have their own home. Therefore, you give them a home in this drawer.

We say that many of you go through life with your experiences and create a miscellaneous drawer within you. You store things. In the beginning, much like that kitchen drawer, it isn't so full, but over time, that drawer fills and you begin to store things that you realize never needed a drawer at all. They never needed a place to be stored. They could have been tossed away a long time ago.

In these times of spring-cleaning, perhaps you look through the drawer and find a key, realizing that you do not even know what this key belongs to. "I don't even remember why I kept this string of rope. I don't even know if these loose batteries rolling about in the drawer are even working. What is this business card sitting in the drawer? I have never heard of this business, so why is it in the drawer?"

You see, you will have no memory of many things in your drawer as far as why they're there or how they belong to you. Your miscellaneous drawer in your kitchen perhaps holds many keys and you do not know which key belongs to which door, so those keys give you no value because there is no understanding to what door they fit. We say that many of you hang on to things in your life, such as keys, for instance, and you really don't remember or you don't know why you hang on to the keys.

You don't know what door which key opens, so there cannot be any value for you. We say there is no need to hang on to things in your drawers if they give you no value. Why hang on to things and create clutter within your drawer, clutter within yourself, by keeping things that hold no value or purpose for you?

There is always a need to have reorganization. There is always a need for spring-cleaning. In your world, you use spring-cleaning to clear out the old and make room for the new, and we say this is a wonderful way to see things. Many of you, however, allow spring to pass without doing your spring-cleaning. You allow another year to pass, and again you do not go through those closets.

The garage becomes fuller, and before you know it, it becomes an overwhelming task! The garage is stuffed with so many boxes filled with things you do not even want to begin to open because the task is now too extreme. We say that for you, it is of great service to not allow your closets, your garages, and your drawers to get so stuffed.

Don't let them fill up in such a way that it becomes overwhelming to the point where you do not wish to put attention there to clear them out. We say that if you can go through life spending each day, each week, or even each month clearing out your drawers and closets, becoming aware of when they begin to get a bit stuffed and going through those items on a more regular basis, you can be aware of what is being stored.

We say that this is how we wish you to treat yourself. Are you holding on to patterns, habits, behaviors, and stories that give you no value? Are you serving yourself well by holding on to these stories you keep boxed inside? Are you serving yourself well by hanging on to the things that really do not hold much purpose for you any longer? Why do you keep clutter within you?

We say that this reorganization time is for you to declutter, to open the closets within you and begin to look at some of the patterns you have and some of the habits you have formed. Take a hard look at some of the conversations and decide if these ways give you any value. "How are these old stories serving me? Did they ever serve me? How do I feel when I speak of these stories?"

Do they not feel good but you share them anyway because you hold on to this pattern of conversation? Perhaps it simply just became a part of what you do. When you go to your miscellaneous kitchen drawer and search for random things, what you find is just that, a bunch of random things, none that really have a home, and we say they are not meant to have a home.

They are random things that do not need a home. If you look in that drawer and you see a pattern of multiple things that go together, then you can perhaps see that those items may need an actual space in the closet. Do you understand what we mean here?

We say that you spend a lot of time throwing a bunch of experiences into a drawer, not really paying attention to whether they hold any real value for you at all. You just do not want to discard them, so you create space within you and hang on to them, and we want to say to you that not all things need a drawer, a closet, or a space in the garage.

Sometimes they need to be thrown away. Therefore, spring-cleaning is an opportunity for you to open those closets, drawers, and garage and look at what have you been storing and see if any of those things have served you well since you stored them. If you can say they have not served you well, then you can say that it is now time to throw them away and clear out your drawers.

This includes unnecessary experiences you hang on to, emotions you hang on to, and understanding that you had those experiences to experience them, but not all experiences are meant to be stored and kept. It is time to spring-clean and look at those items within, and we say to do it with a light heart and step into this project with excitement.

What will you uncover in those drawers? What will you uncover as you begin pulling things out of your inner closet? Do not be attached to those things you find. Simply ask yourself, "Has this served me well? Has hanging on to it been of value to me? Could this space within me be used better? Is this space within me best served hanging on to things that give me no value and no joy—or is now time to make more room within to allow better things in that do give me value, where I can feel joy and have experiences that are indeed worth storing?"

It is important to go through this inner spring-cleaning just like this, asking, "Has it served me or not? Is there a need to keep this within me or isn't there? Do I know where this key fit or not? If I do not, then why am I hanging on to it?" If it is a key from a home from a long time ago, why hang on to it? You no longer have that home with that door, so why keep the key?

Perhaps you no longer are that person who had that experience. As you are looking at your inner closet, you need to say, "I am no longer that person. I no longer live there, and this key is no longer of value to me. So we say that as you go through your spring cleaning, allowing yourself to have this exercise and you are pulling things out of your inner drawer and closet, understand that some of these things you find may make you feel uncomfortable, have given you pain, have made you not feel good about who you are—experiences that made you question yourself and maybe even made you feel small.

And we say it is very much like the key in the drawer—to recognize that those experiences that made you feel these ways that you have been storing were in your past. That key was attached to a home that you no longer live in, so there is no value hanging on to that key, for you do not live there. We say it's similar to these experiences that make you feel in a way that allows you to feel less than you could, not as bright as you should be, not as confident as you are intended to be.

We say that those are the very things you must let go of and that you should remove those things from your drawers. As you do, just as when you clear away at a closet and reorganize it, it feels good. As you clear out your internal drawers and closets and remove the clutter that serves you no purpose, gives you no value, has you feeling heavy in your heart, and no longer resonates with you, whether that be your habits, stories you tell, beliefs that no longer resonate, as you release, toss away, and clear out these things, it will feel very good to you.

You will feel better with those closets reorganized, and your miscellaneous drawer will have far fewer items in it, and we say to do this always with the intention to feel better. Do this exercise with the mindset of clearing out things to feel lighter, we say, and with more space to allow for new and better things, new and better experiences, new and better belief systems that resonate more with who you are today, not from the home from where you once lived, for you are in a new place, a new home, and with it, you have a shiny new key.

Keep the home within you where you reside clean, cleared, and decluttered, for that is the only key you should hang on to. Never allow it to end up in your miscellaneous kitchen drawer.

We hope this helps you.

It is so. Until next time, there is great love for you here.

Edgar

Being Aware

‖‖

Good morning Edgar.

What would you like to make us aware of today?

Ah, yes, it is a fine day and a fine word you use to ask us this. You ask us what we wish you to be aware of. We say this is very good. We simply wish for you to be aware, to be aware of all that is around you. What are you drawn to in your day? You see, there is data there for yourself. Do you ever wonder when you become aware of something? Say, for instance, a woman and her orange blouse. It catches your eye. Do you ever wonder why it caught your eye?

Do you wonder why it was the women wearing the orange blouse and not the one two feet next to her wearing the green one? Do you ever wish to understand what made you aware of it and why?

We say that there are always reasons that your soul is drawn to something. Many of you just take notice of it and do not dig deeper. We say that it would be much better if you would become aware of the woman in the orange blouse and then ask yourself why you are drawn there. To dig deeper. What was it about that color that took your focus to it?

We say to then feel for a moment. What is it about the color orange? How does orange make me feel? What has been my connection to orange in my life? Does it remind me of something or someone? If so, what and whom? Do you get data? Do you think this is a beautiful color?

Is it a happy color for you? Do you have any of this color in your life? If so, where in your life is it placed? When was the last time you wore something orange? How would it make you feel if you wore orange? Would you feel different? What colors do you usually wear? What is the meaning of the color orange? Is there information for you in that color? We say that there is.

You see, life speaks to you all day. Are you hearing? Life does not only speak to you through words and experiences. Life also speaks to you through images, through feelings, and through color. When you become focused upon someone or something, do an exercise with yourself to pause and take the focus inward and become a bit deeper in thought about it. There is where you shall uncover more about you; it is so. There you will find data.

Life is bringing you ways to uncover more about you all day long; you just are not listening. This orange blouse is a simple example. It can be anything. It can be in the sound of someone's voice, a particular flower you see, certain song lyrics you hear as you enter a space that draws your focus to it, a certain conversation that you overheard and have now became focused on it.

Why? Why that conversation? What was it about that conversation that got your attention, and why did you choose to be aware there as opposed to another conversation going on around you? You see, there is data floating all around you. It is that many of you find yourself a bit bored, not having much interest in anything or anyone.

We say that there should never be a case where you feel this way, for there is communication surrounding you and wanting your attention to engage you. Life is wanting to get you to interact with it. But do you? Most of you do not. It can be so fun for you, but instead you stay with your own regular rituals and become a bit rigid in your way of living in life—and we say that life is always talking to you to give you more to play with.

Do you speak back to it? Do you interact with it? Can you go out today and when you become focused upon something ask yourself *why*? Why was this my focus of attention? What is it wanting to show me? Can I have curiosity? What is it wanting to say to me? I want to know.

What is it trying to teach me about myself? I want to learn about me. You see, there is never a reason to be bored when you approach life from this place, the place of becoming aware, and then move toward it and engage yourself with it. This is wonderful.

This will add many colors to your life to get your attention, so you may want to ask the questions so that you can have a vibrant life. For when you ask, dear ones, you always receive the answer. So play with the idea of taking your focus deeper, to become aware and to play a bit with wanting to understand the meaning of why you chose to be aware there and not somewhere else.

There is precision with your focus. Know this. There is no accident with what you become focused on. Does this make you curious? Can you see if you can play and have fun with all the different things you are being made aware of and ask within yourself, *Why was it that and not something else that got my attention?*

It shall give you a fantastic inner reference book for yourself. This, we say, is perfect.

It is so. Until next time, there is great love for you here.

Edgar

Stepping into the Right Shoes in Life

Indeed, we enjoy making the time to be here with you in this way. We like it so much that it is also a time that you enjoy being here in this way. It is so.

There are many things to speak of, many things to have conversations about. What we wish to say is that everything we wish to step forward to speak of is to help you each along a bit on your journey. It is a marvelous journey if you can see that it is.

Not all see that it is a gift given to you, being here in this way, at this time, and with these exact circumstances. Many feel that a journey needs to be wonderful and filled with only positive things. We say that even in the times that feel troublesome, there are positive things, for each journey has positive aspects for self.

We wish to light up the path you are walking on, to help lead you down the road where you can see light, as many walk down their path in life not seeing the light. Therefore, we come forward to do just that. To guide you on your path. To be the lights along your path. To have you focus upon things that will have you feeling better. To give you ideas and things to ponder, things that can percolate within you, things that get you feeling more at ease within yourself so that the next time you come upon a struggle on your path, you will see it differently. Brighter indeed.

We wish to speak regarding your path on your journey in life, to focus on the shoes on your feet. Please understand that we explain it this way in order to express it for you in an easy way. As you are walking down your path, there are many types of shoes that can be placed upon your feet.

We say that the shoes on your feet can play a very important role in how you indeed step onto your path on your journey of life and how you feel while traveling on it. You see, some of you walk on your path completely filled with anticipation, excitement, and joy, and we say that you are wearing the right shoes for yourself. You have put the right shoes upon your feet to walk your path, which feels very good. It does not feel good to wear uncomfortable shoes. Can you understand?

Wearing shoes that do not fit makes it difficult to walk through life, you see. Your feet are always slipping out of your shoes. Do you understand what we say here?

Many of you are just hanging on each day. You always feel as if you are slipping out of your shoes. You are not feeling right with yourself. It is you indeed not having the right fit on your shoes. There are many shoes in many styles and sizes available to you. Life offers many opportunities to give you experiences that you want.

What we wish to say here is that many of you choose to step into your day wearing shoes that do not fit you properly as to who you are, and you wonder why you struggle through the day. Not getting through a day as easily as you could or having better feeling experiences for yourself in your day.

It is difficult to walk through any day with shoes that don't fit. If they are too small, they hurt your feet and prevent you from walking comfortably, and if they are too big for your feet, it is challenging to walk through life also. You need to have the correct size shoe on your foot.

Many of you do not pay enough attention about what shoes you are wearing at all. In many situations, you also do not wear shoes that even belong to you. They are someone else's shoes. You step in your life being someone you are not supposed to be, showing up in life in a way that is not comfortable to you.

We say that this is very much like your wearing shoes that do not fit you, do not feel right to you, and are not a style you like, so there is no desire's filling you. The shoe analogy we express here is about authenticity. Authenticity is wearing shoes that feel right on your feet.

Wearing a style of shoe that feels quite right to you is also important. When you are authentic to who you are, it is you choosing shoes that fit you well. It is then when you step into your day with much more happiness. You then take steps on your path with far greater ease, you see. It feels right for you.

Think for a moment what the shoes look like on your feet. Have you been wearing combat boots, boots that are heavy and clunky? Are your days, as a result, feeling heavy and clunky to you? Are you feeling you are always fighting battles?

Are you wearing flip-flops upon your feet and feeling free and lighthearted as you step into your life? Do you feel this way? Do you wear heels that are very high and give you a backache in your body, knowing that these shoes are not good for you?

You know they give your body pain, but you wear them anyway just because they look good. This is your keeping up appearances, showing up in your life the way others expect to see you, and we say that sometimes this is the case. It is important for you to wear shoes in life that fit you, feel good to you, and allow you to go through life with greater ease.

Each of these types of shoes gives a different experience to you. We wish you to think about the shoes you wear and the experiences you are having when wearing them. Are they clunky? Are they heavy? Do they hurt your feet? Do they cause you pain in your body? Have you experienced these feelings in your life? Are these experiences that you want?

Do you walk around in life with shoes too big for you and then wonder why you get frustrated as you try to walk through your day? Are you putting too much responsibility on your plate each day, never having time for yourself? Are you creating things in your life that keep you always working and hustling and never really enjoying? Have you been slipping out of your shoes and out of joy? Do you feel sometimes that you have boots on your feet? Your feet feel heavy; they hurt from the heaviness of the shoes and needing to lift them with each step you take. Does this make you tired?

This too is how you feel stepping onto your path in life when there are always things you feel must get done. You never rest. It makes you feel heavy and tired. In these moments, are you wearing heavy boots?

There is great value for you to choose to step on your path wearing shoes in life that fit you and not wearing shoes that belong to someone else. Some of you do indeed wear shoes that belong to someone else. You are living your life the way someone else tells you to live it, wearing shoes that do not fit you.

Sometimes you walk through life experiencing things not of your choosing but of someone else's choosing for you—how someone else feels and thinks your life should be and deciding for you how to experience it—and you listen. It doesn't feel right, but you listen and go along with it anyway.

This is you wearing shoes that do not belong to you. This is you placing other people's shoes on your own feet. It does not resonate with you if you are one who enjoys tennis shoes and someone in life keeps telling you to wear shoes with great high heels. You do not like high heels. You resonate with tennis shoes, but you place the heels upon your feet anyway because you want to please, and then you go through life with a backache, you see. You feel pain within the body because you chose to do what does not resonate with or feel right within you. When this occurs repeatedly, you become a bit of a pleaser to others, you see. May we ask you each if you ever choose to please yourself? When you put the tennis shoes on, how does that feel opposed to the heels? Do you understand what we say to you here?

What we wish to express to you is that if you can step into your day paying attention to your own feet, and if you can decide at the start of each day as you dress that you will put on shoes that feel good to you, that resonate with you and are comfortable to you, that you wear shoes that fit wonderfully on your feet, you will have a far better day. This is you being authentic to yourself and choosing to move through your day with yourself, your needs, and your feelings in mind and as priority.

Putting on shoes that fit you and are a style you like feels good to you. This is you pleasing yourself. You are selecting the shoes that will give you better experiences for self as you walk on your life path. Wearing someone else's shoes that are not your style or fit can also be you taking on the load of others when it is not your load to carry.

This is you wearing what does not belong to you either. Sometimes, as you wear other people's shoes long enough, you begin to throw on their coats as well. You become the shopper in someone else's closets. You take on the burdens of others. Now you're walking on your path in life wearing shoes that are not in a style that resonates with you, adding on more to you of what does not fit you. You step in life not yourself. In time, you begin to lose a sense of who you are, you see.

You are one who likes tennis shoes, but instead you throw on those heels and walk on your path with a back that hurts. When you step into life this way, you begin to start carrying more things on you that do not belong to you, do not fit you. We call these coats, throwing on coats of others one after another. All are different sizes, but none are your size and are not meant for you to wear, yet you put them on anyway, and as you do, you take the burdens from others and place them on you. It becomes harder to walk. When you live life this way, it will be quite difficult to walk your path in the joy intended for you, you see.

It is important that each morning as you dress, you are lacing up the shoes that feel good for you. What are those shoes for you? Do you know? What are those feelings you want to express? What are those experiences you want to have? How do you wish to show up and walk in your life? What does that look like for you?

This is a wonderful analogy for you to do each morning. Ask yourself which shoes you are going to wear today. "Am I wearing shoes that are someone else's? Will I be taking on burdens of others? Will I be authentic to myself today and find joy in my life that feels good to me?"

Will I be walking down my path today with my feet hurting or my feet feeling comfortable? What shoes am I going to be wearing today? What shoes feel most comfortable for me? By the shoes you decide to wear, you will know how your day will be for yourself.

You can all understand that wearing shoes that do not feel good straightaway hurt within hours and you want to take those shoes off. Sometimes you are placed in situations in life where you cannot take off those shoes. You have allowed yourself to step into other roles and you are in other people's lives, living within their dramas and other people's situations, and you begin to carry the emotions of them, and here are those coats, you see.

Wearing another person's stuff will never fit or feel right, you see. You must remove them. We use the shoe analogy here to make you aware, and it is something to think about at the start of your day. To feel within you what the shoe analogy means to you personally. It will be different for each of you.

Then ask, "What shoes am I wearing? Are these mine or are they someone else's? Am I wearing my stuff or am I wearing another people's stuff? If you are wearing shoes that belong to someone else and you start your day this way, you can be assured that your day will give you feet that hurt."

If you can dress yourself for the day aware of your choices in shoes and put on the shoes that are comfortable to you, this is you making decisions that are good for you. Preparing yourself to step into your day and on your path, moving in a way that allows you greater ease, is very nice.

Start knowing the power of each of your steps. There may be many shoes in your closet currently, and we say it is time to look at them more closely and begin to remove the ones that do not resonate with who you are or do not feel good to you. Remove from your closet what causes pain to you, holds burdens on you, and gives you unwanted feelings. Discard the shoes that are not yours. Keep the ones that are.

Wear shoes in your day that feel comfortable to you and only you, understanding what is comfortable to you. Know and understand that as you place shoes on your feet that are not yours, they will not feel right and will create pain within your feet, within you, which will not allow you to walk through life in the way you are meant to. Be willing to change your shoes.

Know which shoes fit you, know what shoes do not, and worry not what other people think about what your shoes look like. You know what your shoes must look like and feel like, for they are your feet. It is your life. Nobody knows what feels good on your feet but you. Nobody knows what a comfortable fit for you but you. No one else can ever know this. Do you agree?

Think a little about this. We love stepping forward here, giving you little nuggets of things to consider. We thank you for this time and opportunity to be with each of you this way.

It is so. Until next time, there is great love for you here.

Edgar

Allow Yourself to Receive

Indeed, it is nice to sit here and once again be in this way. It is important to understand that we are always together, for there is never a time that we are not together. We wish to make you aware of this. Coming together in this way, in this moment, is a lovely opportunity for us to work together in yet another way.

The work that we do is of great value for bringing value to others that uplift others is our greatest desire, and we love very much that it is your greatest desire too. Therefore, making time to be in this way to do just that is of great value. So please know and understand as you sit this way that it is bringing great value to others and great value to our work together, you see, strengthening us as well, and it is important to highlight that.

These letters from spirit are quite nice, aren't they? We see and feel the interaction that transpires from across the screen. The excitement, anticipation, joy, and value that it gives to many is a very nice way of being together this way, to bring value to one another. It has been a very nice thing to see how others are now beginning to dig a bit deeper within themselves, beginning to make changes for themselves, and beginning to step into life a bit differently. It is very nice indeed.

We sit here today to ponder on a topic for those of you who come together to listen to our words for you. We wish to speak about making time "to be for self," for making the time to be for self is a very important thing, and we say many people feel that meditation is a way to be with self and to be of service for self, which is true.

But coming together too, and listening to words being expressed, can create great healing for you, you see, so coming together and gathering together for letters from spirit is a wonderful way to be available for self as well, and it is important to highlight this, we say.

Coming together for letters from spirit is a great way for you each to just sit and allow yourselves to be. To sit and allow yourself to receive. Many people do not sit and allow themselves to receive. You are possibly always giving and doing, and here we come forward to allow you simply to sit, to be and to receive. Isn't that nice?

Some of you are now finding these letters quite lovely indeed. Enjoy this time to simply sit and receive the words and the messages within the words for you, to receive the energetic flow that is meant to reach you, touch you so it may lift you, and this is very nice.

Please understand as you sit for these letters from spirit that it is you allowing yourself to be here for you. And we say it is important to highlight this and say bravo for making yourself available for yourself. This is a beginning step to uncovering more for yourself, you see, and so today we wish to have you sit as we speak a bit for you about this.

How often do you make time for yourself? How often do you sit and allow yourself to receive? This is for you to think about. How many times in life have there been those who have wanted to help you and you have turned it down? Others wanting to help you in a way but you not allowing or accepting of it, wanting to do it all yourself?

You see, sitting here allows you the opportunity to know and understand what it feels like to receive, and we say there have been many times in your life when others have wanted to give to you and perhaps you did not allow it. You are becoming so used to being there for everyone else, being there to fix it all yourself, doing it all yourself, and you have become a bit uncomfortable allowing yourself to receive.

Therefore, sitting here for letters from spirit allows you to receive; it's an opening of the gates within here to become more of a receiver in your own life. It is necessary to receive, for it never truly feels good in life only to give and not to ever receive. Would you agree?

Many of you wish to have had somebody, some support, somewhere where there could be a way for others to be giving for you, doing for you, helping you, supporting you, but then there is this inner feeling of your not wanting to accept it, you see, and we wish to open this door for you. To allow you the opportunity to know how it feels to sit and receive. To allow yourself a moment to be giving to yourself, whether it is you doing this in the way we are now or whether it is you simply saying, "Yes, I will receive that help you offer me. Yes, I will accept your invitation to help me in this way rather than declining the invitation that certain people have given me in life."

Many of you have been guilty of declining the invitation of help, not wanting to take the hand being offered to you. We say that doing this cuts off the receiving end for you, you see, for there must be an energetic exchange in life, you giving and you also receiving.

There is no true energetic flow in life when there is only giving and never receiving. There must be this flow that allows this movement to come, you see. And when you have this movement of energetic exchange of "I am giving to you, and I too am accepting the return of giving back to me," this is a wonderful way of being, the right way of being. And many of you do not feel it is right to accept what is trying to be returned to you for you. We say that it would be nice for you to see it differently, to understand that by your not allowing others to be giving to you, it cuts off their energetic flow as well as yours, you see. It hinders you and them. When you are one who gives, it feels good, does it not? This is why you wish to give. You like to be that one who makes a difference. You like to be that one who helps.

You like to be that one who fills her plate. It is nice to do that, but when you constantly fill your plate and never allow someone to take from that plate for you, it then becomes a heavy plate because energy is not flowing, no energetic flow that gives harmony and balance.

It is important for you all here now to understand that there is an energetic balance necessary for you. Therefore, sitting here now allows you to have that energetic flow of receiving, and it feels very good. Coming forward at this day and at this time to sit and listen and to have this interaction and this exchange feels good, and many look forward to this time because it feels good to receive. Understand that this is you receiving and it feels good. It feels nice. It is because there is an energetic flow. You are showing up to allow yourself to receive the words that we express and wish to give to you. Energy is flowing nicely.

If you can step into your day a bit thinking about the ways you are an open door, always giving to others in all the different circumstances and situations and experiences you have in which you do, you can now understand how it creates a flow of energy outward. However, when you do not allow your door to stay open to allow a flow of energy to come back to you, it cuts off the energy flow.

There must be an energetic exchange, we say. There must be the flow of energy to have harmony and balance in your life. How many of you can sit here now and think of a time when guidance, support, or help was offered to you and you turned it down? Someone offered a hand to you to help you in a situation and you said, "Oh, no, I am okay. That's not necessary.

How many of you have been living just being that solo warrior, giving it all, handling it all, and not receiving at all? When you do this repeatedly you begin to feel heavy inside yourself. You begin to feel off because the energy is not flowing and there is no harmony. However, if you can be both the giver and the receiver, you see, then there is energetic flow creating your balance and your harmony within you.

Imagine now for a moment, your eyes closed and you holding your hands up high, a hand on the left and a hand on the right. The hand on your left is receiving, and the hand on your right is giving. The hand on your left is closed, and the hand on your right is open. Your giving hand is always open, but the receiving hand is closed. The closed hand is unable to receive harmony and balance, and in time, you become off and empty feeling because you have not allowed energy to flow through you as it is intended to give you the harmony within you. To give you balance.

Your door not being open to allow energy to move through you now gives blocked energy, which is not how energy can be. It must move. There is an energetic exchange that everybody needs. Moreover, not allowing others to give to you hinders your energetic flow as well as theirs, you see. If you can feel into "I want to be a giver," you must also understand the need to allow others to give to you.

Allowing them to give to you gives them the energetic flow and harmony for themselves. One needs another. You are here to work together. There is a need for one another. A wonderful exchange can only be done together.

Oftentimes, you feel you want to go about it solely, and we say that one needs another. There must be an exchange of giving and an exchange of receiving. Many of you have been such wonderful givers and terrible receivers.

We love you stepping in this way at this time of our letters. See yourself now in this very moment, as you have made time to be here for yourself, on this day and at this exact time, to absorb this data, this information, this communication, this flow of energy intended for you. In this particular moment, you are a receiver. Isn't that wonderful?

Don't you sit here now and feel good in this flow of energy during these letters? It is because you have opened the door and allowed the harmony of energy to flow in and out of you. This is very nice. We wish to put a little flashlight here for you to understand the importance of being a receiver of self.

We say that there are so many of you trying to do it all alone, to do things by yourself, to be separate, and we say it has never been intended to be that way. A giver needs to receive. A giver needs to be a receiver as well. The energetic field within you to give asks from it to receive also.

As you give, it is the energy moving out, and then energy needs to return. Are you allowing that energy to return to you so you can have harmony and balance? We ask you to ponder that a bit. Think back to all the times someone wanted to give you a hand and you declined the hand. How many times somebody offered you a voice and you did not want to have the conversation. How many times have you been somewhere, and someone offered to help you with your bags, and you said "No, not necessary? I have this."

You see, receiving comes in many forms. It is energy exchange, and energy come in many forms. It can be someone helping you with your groceries. It can be helping you with words through conversation that you were not open to have but you needed to have that opening to express your feelings. It could be someone offering to lighten the load of chores, such as unloading a dishwasher.

There are many ways that an exchange of energy can come back to you to give balance to you. It is very important for you to understand that it is necessary. It is necessary for your well-being to be a receiver as well as a giver.

How many ways in life would you wish to be a receiver? How many ways can you think of when you could have used some receiving? A voice or a hand to receive from? To sit and allow yourself to receive as you are now?

Perhaps it has shown up for you but you turned it away; in that moment of turning it away, you cut yourself off from the energetic flow from it. We just wish you to understand that there is great value for you in life to have harmony by allowing yourself to be a receiver. Many of you feel bad being a receiver; you only wish to be the giver, and we say that can never be good.

You must be the giver, and you must be the receiver. And this must be every day. Think of all the ways you are a giver. Think of all the ways you put out that energy of giving and how many times energy was returning and flowing back to you but you closed the door to it, feeling you are to give only.

In the moment of you shutting the door of the flow returning to you, you cut the energy off from both you and the individual wanting to be a giver to you. There is a purpose to why you give, and it is to allow another the opportunity to do it as well. A giving is always an exchange.

Life is always flowing with giving. There is you giving and then someone else needing to give to you, and then you need to give to something and then something is needing to be given back to you. Nature is giving to you every day. In that sense, you are always receiving, are you not? Nature is always giving to you experiences and ways to receive.

You can sit in the sunlight, and in that instance, you are receiving from nature. You receive the feeling of the sun feeling good upon your body. You receive vitamin D for your nutrition. You are receiving. You have no trouble with receiving from nature, thankfully, we say. However, when it comes to individuals, many have great trouble with this.

You must understand that there is a flow in nature to give, just as there is a need and flow in all individuals to give. If you can be a receiver of nature and allow feeling the breeze upon your face, allow the sun to shine upon you, and allow the experience of nature giving to you easily, with no questioning of it, but the moment there is an individual in life wanting to be a giver, you then stop and question it. You resist it and think, *Oh, no, I must not accept that hand.*

Think of everyone as nature. You have no trouble accepting the gift of giving from nature, and you should not have trouble accepting the gift of giving from others, we say. Do you see what we mean here?

We wish to just say to you that many times your energy feels blocked, and we say many times that you block your own energy unnecessarily, only because you do not allow yourself or do not feel worthy in yourself of wanting to receive. We say that this hinders you. We wish very much for you to look at it differently.

We bring this forward in this way because many of you here like to give but not receive, and if you can understand that as you give and allow others to give back to you and allow yourself to receive, you are indeed giving again, you see.

Therefore, for you that are out there who are those givers, you must understand that as you become a receiver, you allow others to be givers, which creates energetic flow. Can you see? This is giving again. We want you to step into your day in a way that feels lighter.

We wish for you to understand that there is great joy in you giving and there is also great joy in allowing them to give to you. When you can have this energetic exchange back and forth, there is movement and flow, and then there are no blocks.

When you have blocks, you have buildup. When you have buildup, you then have energy that is within you, not allowing itself out, and this feels pent up, which is why you feel heavy, with too much on your plate.

You are not allowing yourself to have the energy to flow through you and for you. We wish to step forward today to give you a new way of seeing this, that you are always giving, even when you are receiving. There is a giving-ness within each of you as you receive and allow, and we say "allow" because it is up to you to allow.

If you can allow nature to give to you by having you sit and receive the sun shining upon your face, you are allowing this, for you could sit indoors. It is a decision. Step out in nature and allow it to give you the sounds and the scents and the feeling. This is you allowing nature to give to you. We wish you to think of it this way when you think of others.

When you are stepping into your day and your plate is full, and you're feeling heavy and needing of support, and someone offers a hand or an opportunity presents itself for you to receive help, make sure your door is open to allow the energy to flow and move and know that energy moving toward you is you still giving as well. Yes?

We know that this will help you, and we know that many of you struggle with this a bit. Therefore, we come forward here to be light and to give a topic for you to ponder and to understand that you are a beautiful, giving being.

There are opportunities wanting to come to you that allow you ways to receive help for you in life, if you allow them to. Sometimes this comes in circumstances, sometimes this comes in opportunities, sometimes it comes in experiences and sometimes in people, but are you saying yes to the circumstances, experiences, opportunities and the people wanting to give for you? Are you allowing yourself to be a receiver?

We say now that some of you will begin to. We say that this is the case because you sit here now in this way to receive the words we express for you here. As the words seep within, you too will understand more of the importance in you becoming the receiver. It allows you to give. It allows you to receive. There is this ebb and flow of this marvelous energy always wanting to be expressed.

It is always your doing and choosing whether you allow it or not. There will be far greater harmony within your life if you choose to allow. Yes?

Think on this a bit. Try this a bit. The next time you feel your plate is full, your boots heavy, your heart weighted, and you see an opportunity that can lighten it, instead of turning away from it, open the door and let the opportunity in. When someone offers you a hand, instead of declining it, understand by accepting it that you are allowing them to be a giver, you see, and you too are allowing yourself to be a receiver; this exchange is a wonderful energetic flow that will always feel better for both you and them.

It is so.

We love your being here listening to our words that we hope seep within you. We wish your heart to be light, your inner door always to be open, and we wish you to live in joy, as this is how you were intended to be. To have energetic harmony is indeed a way to have joy.

It is so. Until next time, there is great love for you here.

Edgar

The Planter Box

Indeed, a good day to you all. It is lovely to be together in this way. Do you agree? Having this opportunity to be of service to others in the way that we can, together here. And you being in service to self by sitting here now with us.

As we sit here today and prepare for a new letter from spirit, we must take just a moment to allow you the knowing of what is transpiring. We like that those are stepping into each Monday excited, excited for the discovery of what will be; joining us here; and us traveling you each down new waters—waters with new ways of being, new ways of seeing things, new ways of being able to open your hearts, new ways of allowing yourselves to be more. More of who you are.

What shall we speak about? We say that it is always important for one to understand who they are; and many do not begin the day with an energetic place that is serving for them, you see.

Therefore, we say today that we'd like to speak a bit about your own energetic place. How are you setting your energy up for the day? How are you stepping into your day? Know and understand that you each are growing, whether you see it or not. Each of you has growth and change within you every day. For that growth and that change to occur in the way that you wish, it is important that you have the energetic place within you and that you set yourself and your energy in the way each day to allow the growth to be. Understand that you are land because truly that is what you are, your soul being land. Think a moment of yourself as a planter box.

Now, your land has no limitations of walls. However, we want just to put focus here so you can have a starting point. Therefore, we place you here now to imagine a box. A bit of a planter box, you see, and as you have this planter box, your box, you can plant and grow whatever it is you wish, for it is your box, your land.

With you being the land and the planter box, what do you wish to plant? It would be nice for each of you to start each day a bit this way, choosing your seeds. What shall I be planting today? Your land within you is always wanting to have a harvest, you see. Understand that you are this lovely planter box and you are the one in control and in charge of what is planted within it.

As you step out into your day, every day, we say to be mindful of this planter box that is you, knowing and understanding that it is for you to decide what is going to be planted in your box each day. When you have a planter box and you wish to plant anything at all, one must prepare the soil, you see, your soul being the soil.

You must allow your soul to be able to express itself when you have a planter box and you're wishing to plant tomatoes, cucumbers, carrots. We use vegetables and fruits here but it could be anything. We'll say vegetables, as you all understand that vegetables are good for you. That gives you an understanding that what you plant must be good for you.

Therefore, we'll plant cucumbers, asparagus, and other vegetable, whatever is to your liking. Your planter box is to plant and grow what is good for you. You must tend to the soil. Every farmer and every gardener prepare the soil for the seeds they wish to plant.

You are no different, for you are each gardeners and farmers as well. A gardener, when wanting to garden, knows and understands the importance of tending to the soil and preparing it for what is desired to be planted within it. A farmer knows and understands that as they begin to plant their crops, they must tend to the soil as well.

And we say that all of you are planting seeds each day. As you are planting seeds within the land that you are, again we'll call it a planter box. We ask you, "Are you tending to the soil or are you just throwing the seeds all around with no care toward how the seeds can grow?"

We say that tending to the soil is very valuable for you. Begin your days with the mindset of tending to your soil, understanding that every day you're a gardener and it is always in the gardener's decision of what it is you are planting, which seeds you're allowing to grow.

Are you allowing those seeds to grow within the best soil possible to have the greatest growth for you? We say that many of you do not see it this way. Many of you do not see that. In fact, you each go about your day not paying much attention to how you start your day and all the seeds that you drop.

Your soil needs tending to as you begin each day. Are you giving yourself what you need to begin your day in the right way? Are you allowing yourself to tend to your soil to allow yourself to have the type of soil that will produce the harvest, the crop, the vegetables in the healthiest way possible for your life?

As a gardener, as you plant your carrots and your cucumbers, there should be anticipation within you, should there not? Anticipation for those seeds to materialize into those carrots or in those cucumbers growing. As you plant a garden, you have visions within you, hopes within you, desires for those seeds to achieve their potential, to allow those vegetables to express themselves as they are meant to, and you have excitement for that.

Do you step into your day with excitement of what it is you plan to express each day? We say that if the soil is not tended, you are not stepping into the day in the right mindset. You will then begin to plant, yes, but you will plant within soil that is not ready to produce the outcome of what you hope. These are your hopes, wishes, dreams, and desires.

Do you see what we mean? You can think of yourself as the soil, you see, and you always need to tend to it. When you tend to the soil that is

111

you, in the way that feels good to you and that is right for you, it is then when you begin the start of every day tending to your own soil. You then can have an absolute knowing that you shall be producing that which is good for you.

And as you have a mindset of stepping into your day doing what's right for your soil, creating soil that is healthy for you so you can produce healthy vegetables, healthy experiences, healthy choices, you see, you then grow experiences in your day that replicate and respond to the soil that you have created. You see that your seeds will create an outcome in accordance with the soil it is set in.

If you can understand that each day you should step into it as that farmer or as that gardener, knowing that you are that land and you are choosing each day, how you plant, you're choosing what you plant and you are choosing the soil in which you're planting. The outcome of those seeds, the outcome of what you plant, is determined by the care of the soil.

We say that if you can begin your days tending to your own soil, nurturing the soil, you will have a far greater harvest to enjoy. What does it mean to nurture the soil? Well, it means doing things that feel right for you and doing things that feel good to you and not doing things that do not. It is choosing to make a decision to actually work within that soil, you setting down the foundation for yourself to have a nice day.

As you sit with the intent and you step into your day, with a mindset of tending to your soil properly, you will then deliberately make choices that are good for you. With each decision that you're making, you will then have a connection with you tending to your soil. Lifting the soil, mending and sowing that soil, preparing it for what can be.

As you step into the day with more of a positive mindset, you shall have a more positive mindset when you're caring for the soil, the soil being you, because that feels good to you. Whenever you're feeling good to you, you're dropping seeds into your soil, into your planter box, and then you can know and understand that that soil has been tended to correctly and you know that those seeds that are being dropped into your soil, into your planter box, are going to produce healthy vegetables that are good for you.

Many of you do not tend to your soil. Many of you do not place focus and attention here. You begin your days just dropping seeds into dirt that is hard, dirt that has no nutrition for what you wish to grow in your life. You have not prepared the soil.

And you wonder why things are not growing well for you and your life? Why are things not growing well in your planter box, in your life, your planter box being your life, the soil being your soul? As we mentioned, your planter box has no walls, really. However, it's a starting out place, you see, and sometimes we need to take smaller steps toward bigger steps.

We come forward to say to start as a planter box and just start nurture the soil within that planter box. Know and understand that as you prepare the soil, you are preparing your day, and as you are preparing the soil and you are preparing the day, you have now placed yourself in the right mindset.

As you are placing yourself in the right mindset, you have a better energy within you. And as you have a better energy within you, you are now dropping seeds into that soil and now those seeds have healthy soil to grow from. As you do this day in and day out, you will begin to start seeing the seeds grow.

On day one, you shall not see those seeds grow, for they are still being developed, but you can know and understand that although you may not see the changes within you right away, know that they are preparing for growth because you have planted those seeds within soil and you have given the seed every opportunity to grow healthy.

Then you must go about your day and the day ahead, and the day ahead again, giving nutrition to those seeds that you have planted within you through the soil. Seeds need water, and seeds need sunlight. As you plant the seeds and create the harvest and soil that is needed for it to have a healthy start, you then need to be mindful also of your energetic place.

Looking for things that feel good is giving light to your seeds, moving through your day looking for things that put a smile upon your face. Looking for situations and conversations that feel good to you. Avoiding those that don't—that is shade. And you cannot grow healthy vegetables in shade.

You need the sun. Therefore, you need things in your life that reflect the sunlight and light you up. That is, internally giving sunlight to your seeds. Do you see what we mean here? You are a planter box every day.

Every day you are choosing to work with the soil or not, to tend to your seeds or not. And each day as you tend to the soil, making it a priority, say, "I know I will step into my day and seeds will drop into my soil, and I wish so very much to have soil that is healthy. Therefore, I may drop seeds within that soil that can give it what it needs to grow.

Making that attempt is creating positive seeds for yourself, you see, because you're putting attention into what is positive for you, because you're attending to yourself. When you tend to yourself, you're always dropping positive seeds, and although it may take a few weeks before you see the difference, one morning you shall wake up and see what you have sowed because they shall pop through the soil, and you will begin to see the effects of your tending to your soil, and then you will see more and more effects.

Then that sprouting through the soil shall grow and more sprouting will occur. You will feel differently now. Now things will really begin to take shape in your life, and you will feel it. And before long, you will see those beautiful orange carrots, those lovely green cucumbers, or those wonderful lush red tomatoes; you will begin to understand that you have now created a garden for yourself in your own doing because you have made yourself a priority.

Now you're living a life that is healthier because you have planted seeds within you that are healthy for you, and you are happier because you have planted seeds within you that are healthy for you by making decisions that are healthy for you, moving in a direction that feels good to you, being with those who feel good to you being, mindful now always of what feels good to you and what doesn't.

Do you see what we mean? You are sowing your own soil. Tending and caring for your own soil is for you. It must be a priority if you want a life that produces things that are good for you. Everything must start with the soil. Therefore, everything must start with you. Make decisions to make yourself a priority.

Make decisions to tend to your own needs—you must tend to your own wishes and aspirations and desires; you must put focus and attention there, and you must tend to your soil every morning. You must ask yourself, "What am I desiring today? What positive experiences am I looking for today? What wonderful things shall I come across today? What beautiful conversations will move and inspire me today? What shall I seek today? You are then in fact setting the intention of producing healthy seeds within you to add to your garden."

In addition, you are being aware of your soil and treating that soil with care and love, which is being good to you. Do you find a place within yourself where you can be still for just a few moments and just allow that time to be for you? Do you allow yourself to sit quietly? Are you placing things on your calendar that you can be excited about, that you can look forward to?

When you dress in the morning, are you choosing to wear something that feels happy to you? Are you wearing a color that does not? Do you see what we mean here? As you begin your day, do you listen to music in the morning that creates an energy within you that makes you happy? Are you setting your mind in the right place at the start of every day?

This is tending to your soil. Therefore, we wish to say to you here that there is great value for you to see yourself as a gardener. Moreover, many of you who begin to see yourselves as gardeners will begin to grow healthy vegetables within their planter box.

Some of you will find this so marvelous, and you shall feel so good. Now knowing the importance of tending to your soil, it prepares your mindset to drop healthy seeds in your soil every day. As you begin to do this day in and day out, you will begin to see the difference that it makes within your life. You will then begin to see the sprouting out of the soil, you see, and then you shall feel different, you shall move differently, and you shall be excited because you shall now see the rewards of your efforts and will feel different because of it.

Some of you will feel so excited for this that you no longer want to be in that planter box. You now will see yourself more as a farmer and no longer a gardener. Then, in that moment, you have expanded your land because you have now decided to step into the day knowing the great possibilities and that your joy in life is a decision.

Some of you will find great desire in this, and it will make great shifts within you. You will now see yourselves as farmers. You will then grow a fantastic harvest for yourselves, you see. We just wish for you to understand that tending to your soil each day is very, very important and that nothing can grow easily without healthy soil. You must have a healthy mindset.

You must have healthy energy, and you must have healthy desires. This all grows and creates a healthy garden. Ask yourself, "Am I tending to my soil every morning as I start my day? Am I allowing myself to be that gardener for myself? Am I allowing myself to choose and grow things in my life that are good for me, and do I know that it is possible and that it is only a decision of my choosing to do it? Do I choose now to do it? To understand also that you can step into your day this way feeling excited for what you will grow.

Understand that the greatest garden in life is the one that sits within you. If you can be excited for the carrots that you grow in your true garden, your real garden in life, understand that there is a greater garden within you. This is the one you should also always be tending to first—that garden within you—making it a priority at the start of every day so you may get yourself in the right place and space.

As you walk now into your day, you're always dropping seeds into the soil that are good for you. And this indeed is how you create a lovely garden in life, a garden that offers exactly what it is you wish. It is so. Think about this a bit. Think about what you wish to plant in your garden.

Also think about whether you are one that could possibly be the farmer as well. It is exciting to think about, is it not? We say it is indeed, that the possibilities are there for you always. That to grow wonderful things in your life, you must always start with the soil—your soul.

Begin discovering what it is that makes you feel happier. What things can you do that will put a smile on your face? What things have you moved away from that used to give you joy, which you've stepped away from but you can maybe walk toward again? This is all nutrition for your garden. You see, this is all nutrition for your soil. This is the preparation that you need to allow the seeds to grow from within you.

We hope this gives you something to think about, something to ponder, and we wish just to say to you here that you are magnificent gardeners. In addition, so many of you are also magnificent farmers. Whether a gardener, whether a farmer, however big you wish your land to be expanded to, it is all possible, you see.

Seeing yourself this way will give you the expansive land that you wish for. And within that land, you can grow whatever it is that you wish.

It is so.

Think about what you wish to grow. Think about what that looks like. More importantly, think about what that *feels* like. Begin your day starting with the intent of creating just that. Begin to move through life looking for experiences, conversations, people, things, and activities that you are drawn toward, ways of feeling better.

Know that by doing that, you can mentally understand and mentally visualize that these are seeds dropping into your soil because there is growth growing within you. And if you're wishing to have a life of your choosing, a life that is healthy and abundant, understand that the only thing holding you back from having it is you giving care to your soil. It is so.

We thank you for this time and opportunity to be here with you. It is always quite lovely to shine a flashlight here in areas that can get you thinking a bit more.

It is so. Until next time, there is great love for you here.

Edgar

Driving with Your Inner Tires Aligned

It is a wonderful time to share space with all of you in this way. Our intent is to come forward and to bring forward things for you to ponder, to find new ways of seeing yourselves and your circumstances of seeing things in your life.

Oftentimes, you all tend to look at the areas in which things are not going so well for you. Yes, you tend to put focus and attention on areas that are indeed at a place where it is not of your liking, and we say that you seem to spend a lot of time there.

Yes, we say that many of you spend a lot of time focusing in areas that do not give you the feelings that you like, that do not give you the experiences that you like, that do not give you feelings within you that you like.

So today we'd like to speak a bit about focus. Where are you focusing your thoughts? Where are you focusing your attention? Where are you focusing your time? Within these questions that we ask you, you will be able to know more about how your time is spent, you see.

Are we spending time in thoughts that feel good to us? Are we spending time in our day doing things that feel good to us? Are we spending time with those who make us feel good? Are we having conversations and topics that feel good? Are we having thoughts that feel good? Where are you placing your focus?

Are you placing focus in an area that feels uncomfortable, receiving emotions from where you're placing focus that again feels uncomfortable for you? If you always spend time and focus placed in areas that feel uncomfortable, you will receive emotions that feel uneasy and unsettling.

There will always be more coming to you from wherever it is that you're placing focus, and, you see, it is very easy to place focus in any direction.

It is always of your choosing, you see, of where you place your focus, where you place your time, where you put your attention.

We just wish to put a little flashlight here to say that there are so many of you who tend to place your attention in areas that bring you more of things that you do not want. These things can be conversations. These things can be people. These things can be circumstances. These things can be thoughts.

However, thoughts, people, attention, and conversations that don't feel well create more unwell feelings, you see. Therefore, it does not serve you at all to place focus in areas that do not feel well to you. We say here that we wish to give you an understanding that it is always your choice and decision as to where you begin to place your focus.

We understand that sometimes focus lingers and that you may have the intention to try very hard to place focus in areas that feel better, placing attention and time spent in areas that feel good. And then, gradually and slowly, things linger away back to the place that feels unwell. We understand that it is not easy to control your focus, but we say that you have the ability to control and to decide where you place your focus.

We just wish for you to understand that it is always your decision. You may decide to place focus somewhere with the right intention and the right energy and begin the day very well, but by noontime, start to feel a bit differently. This is your indicator that perhaps maybe you have gotten off the road a bit, that perhaps maybe here is where you need to stop and pause and realign your tires.

When you drive a car and you have tires that are unaligned, they take you to the right or they drive you to the left. They do not drive you straight. You all have had tires that had alignment issues. When you drive and let go of the wheel, your car will pivot one way or pivot the other way, but it does not pivot straight.

We say that straight is the way to drive because when you drive straight, you are focused. And when you drive straight, you know you're going to a destination of your liking. However, as you let go of the wheel and you begin to stop paying attention to how you're feeling, you see, you begin to allow those tires to lose the alignment and they start veering off course for yourself, you see.

Do you see what we mean? Think of yourself as the vehicle, you with these lovely tires, starting out your day driving with focus and direction and with clear knowing of where you want to go. Consciously set the intentions of how you wish your day to be and what energy you wish to feel.

You go with the intent to drive straight, hands on the wheel, tires aligned, and then gradually, through the hours of the day, you get a little sidetracked, you see. Conversations show up in your experience, circumstances begin to show up in your experience, and other things begin to need your attention.

And then, in that moment, your hands begin to loosen from the steering wheel and you begin to recognize that the car, now you, is now moving in a different direction than you had indicated. We say that it is very mindful to pay attention to how you feel, for it is your feelings that will allow you to be aware of the alignment of those tires, you see.

When you begin to feel you're being pivoted, moved, and taken off course a bit, that is when you must stop, refocus, redirect, and place your hands back on that wheel, placing your hands back on the wheel, where you again have control. Sometimes unknowingly, your hands just become a little too loose on that wheel.

Sometimes the hand falls short and instead of two hands, there's one. And sometimes there are no hands. Then your experience in the day begins to go in a different direction. Therefore, what we wish to say to you here is always to have a check-in with yourself, to check in with yourself through the day to make sure your hands are always on your own steering wheel.

What we mean by that is to always pause a bit through the day; allow yourself a meter for yourself to just check in with yourself. You place many things on your calendar. You should make a mental note with yourself as well. Plan something every few hours just to sit a moment and say, "How am I feeling?"

Allow yourself every couple of hours just to give yourself thirty seconds. That's all it needs. Thirty seconds is more than enough just to sit and feel into how your day been going so far. Become aware of the feelings that you receive from that question and use them as guiding signals. We say that it's very good and very important to always be asking yourself questions.

Make it a habit, an intention for yourself, to always check in with yourself every few hours to decide if in fact your hands have still been on the wheel, that you have been driving straight, your focus isn't being taken off from that desire of the experiences you're wanting to have, of the energy place that you wish to choose to step into.

If you can, just step in every day and check in with yourself quickly for thirty seconds and just say, "This is my time now. I'm going to give myself thirty seconds to just make sure my tires are aligned, that my hands are on the wheel, and that I am in charge of this vehicle that is me, knowing that I am choosing where I'm driving. And when I take focus off the direction in which I want my life to go today, it is me taking my hands off the wheel. If my car is not driving straight, I know I am not aligned. And I know I am not aligned, my tires are not aligned, by the way I'm feeling."

Therefore, it is wonderful for you to stop, pay attention, and feel into how you begin your day. Get yourself in that energetic place with a full tank, going onto the road with your hands on the wheel with the intention of where you're going, with focus placed in the direction you want to go, with the experiences you want to have, with the energy that you want to step into and move.

Then, every two hours, check in. After thirty seconds, ask, "How am I feeling now?" If you're finding yourself feeling differently than what you intended a few hours prior, you know you are now driving a bit off course.

Your tires are not aligned, the car is pivoting too far to the right or too far to the left, and you're no longer driving straight. That means it is for you now to say, "Time to put my hands back on the wheel, time to take charge of this vehicle that is me, time to renavigate myself straight, you see."

This is a lovely exercise for you to do. When you become this particular exercise a habit, it will become second nature because habits need practice, you see. In the beginning, you need to be very mindful of making the time to do this.

Before long, it will become second nature to you, you see. Moreover, you will always be driving through your day aware of whenever your body is giving you an indication that your hands have now been removed from the wheel.

We say that it would be wonderful for you to begin to make an intention for yourself and give yourself the thirty seconds, every couple of hours, just to check in. *How am I doing? How am I feeling? How has my day been going so far?*

When you recognize that you have gone a little off the road, your hands a little bit off the wheel, your tires feeling a bit unaligned, feeling you have now moved in another direction, you can pause and say, "What happened? What brought me here? What took my hands off the wheel?" That is information and data for you, you see.

It is very important for you to become aware of what things occur in your life that allow you to let your hands slip off the wheel or what slowly and gradually takes you off course. Do you see what we mean?

We are here to shine light with you to say that you are your driver of your vehicle; you are the driver of your car. And it is for you to decide if your hands stay on that wheel or not.

It is for you to decide what direction you are going at the start of every day, and it is for you always to be mindful, just as you do as you drive your real car. You do not take your focus off the freeway, do you?

You stay focused when you are driving. But the moment you daydream, you oftentimes miss the exit. Do you understand? As you go through your day, have the intent to keep your hands on the wheel, in charge of the direction in which you're going, in charge of what you are looking to experience each day. Choose to have feelings that feel better each day, experiences that feel better, conversations that feel better. Keep moving in the direction of things that feel happier to you.

It is always you who chooses that. Understand that when you move away from those feelings and your experiences begin to change, it is only you who are recognizing then that your hands slipped from the wheel. Say, "I am no longer focused in the direction I intended at the start of the day."

It is the same as driving on the highways or the freeways and daydreaming a bit and missing your exit. Then you have to renavigate yourself back and return back to the focus of where it is you are going, and it is the same here, we say.

It will serve you well to know and understand that focus is always necessary in your life. The focusing of how you're feeling is always very important in your life and keeping control of what you are wanting to experience is always for you. Moreover, it is always your choice to decide to do that or not.

You are your own driver, and you may drive down any road you choose. There are many roads in life, life giving you many experiences, many roads to travel down, we say. It is always for you to decide what road feels good to you. This is not something somebody else could ever tell you.

Nobody knows what road is better for you than you, and we are always wanting you to sit with self because it is within yourself that you are always being guided to the road that is for you, you see. And you're always being guided by the emotions that you're feeling within your body.

Your emotions are navigating you toward the road that feels good for you or doesn't feel good for you. And the road that feels good to you is always a result of the emotions that feel good to you, and the emotions that do not feel good to you are always an indicator that you're a bit off road or on a road not meant for you, that you took your hands off the wheel and are now driving a little bit with unaligned tires, you see. But you always have a choice to renavigate yourself back. Just as you drive down the freeway or a highway or a road and you miss your exit, you become aware, do you not? We wish for you to understand that you too can become aware often through the day, to keep you on the road that is right for you, by paying attention to how you are feeling and to make the time to check in on yourself.

We say to check in on yourself because it is within where you hold the feelings, you see. It is within where you know if something feels good or not. It is never externally; it is always internally. So always trust what you feel internally to know the direction of the road that you, the vehicle, is driving down. Always become aware of how you feel.

We say that this exercise would be very helpful for you to keep yourself focused and aligned. Alignment is quite important, is it not? When you are aligned with yourself, you always feel better. And this is why it's important to keep your hands on the wheel. When your hands are on your wheel, you are always aligned.

When you let go of your steering wheel in life, your tires become unaligned, you see, and they go in a different direction than is intended for you. Therefore, we wish to give you this little nugget to think about and process. Yes, we love so much stepping in here and giving you easy ways to help you step into your day.

You are marvelous beings, and you have so many roads in life that you can select and choose from. How exciting. It is always of your picking; it is always of your choosing. Therefore, choose what feels good and always try to stay on the road that is there for you, the one that offers the experiences you want.

Understand that if you are sidetracked, your hands off the wheel, and your tires a bit unaligned, it is always possible to align yourself again. It is always possible to move yourself back to focus, back to your hands on the wheel, by simply having an awareness of it. It is as easy as that.

Every two hours, just begin to give yourself thirty seconds. Do this quick little exercise that will train you to becoming mindful and aware of your feelings through the day. This will help you very much in staying on the road that is right for you.

We love stepping forward here. We love having this engagement. We love being a part of you in this way and sharing easy ways to help you each along. It is our desire to come forward and to help you in the ways we feel will give you a contribution that will add value to you.

It is so. Until next time, there is great love for you here.

Edgar

Finding and Feeling Forgiveness

Indeed, it is always a lovely time to sit here as we create a new letter from spirit. It is so. For as we always say, there is so much that can be spoken about, so much that can be discussed. There is no topic that is not important or not valuable.

And here we say again that it is time for us to gather with you in this most wonderful way to help shine a flashlight toward getting you each to see things a bit differently. Perhaps a bit more clearly. Wanting so much to give you new ways of feeling within you and new ways of feeling about you. This is very important as well, and as we speak about feelings, there is a topic of forgiveness that one has asked us to speak on. We think this is a lovely topic indeed, for there are many where you are who struggle a bit with forgiveness.

Moreover, there are many here where we are who at one time struggled with forgiveness. However, you see, there is no forgiveness needing to be here any longer from where we are. But we do in fact understand that there is still a need to understand forgiveness where you are. Forgiveness can be a very big word, you see, because within it holds many feelings and many degrees of feelings too, we say.

When one is struggling with forgiveness, we say to you, what is the meaning to you? Forgiveness is different things to different people, you see. There are different degrees of forgiveness as well, you see. It is very wide, and it runs very deep. And it has been needed within the hearts of so many.

What we mean by that is not having forgiveness, not being able to feel forgiveness, not being able to know and understand how in fact to have forgiveness when others have wronged you. When we say "wronged," this could be physically or it can be emotionally. For the need of forgiveness also shows up in different forms as well, you understand.

For some of you, it is words that were spoken to you that have hurt you, that have left you feeling weathered, you see. And the effects from that storm of words have held to you quite tightly and it have caused much internal damage within you.

Some of you have had physical circumstances that have made you feel unwilling to forgive. Some of those physical conditions that have happened to you perhaps have lain very deep within you with much emotional damage.

Some of these happened early on, when you were a child, you see, and for others, it came later. However, whether it came later or whether it was early, it has in fact created storms within you, storms that have not allowed you to recover from them, you see.

Here you sit and wonder how to forgive those who have created such turmoil within you, such storms within you. We can say we understand that there is pain, that there is pain that others have caused you that has prevented you from having or being able to find forgiveness within you.

We say that you are not wrong. We say that you are not wrong for feeling how you feel, for when someone wrongs you, causes pain within you, and gives you something within you that has changed your landscape, it has prevented you from being able to move ahead or move forward in your life. We understand that it is hard to forgive because there's been a sense of you that a piece of you within has become lost in that storm, you see, which some of that storm has taken from you. And what we really truly want to say to you, to ask you, is whether forgiveness is really about needing to forgive that person or if it's about finding that peace within you that was taken?

What is it for you? That is a very important question to ask yourself, you see. For some of you, it is just no longer having that that was taken from you, and that is where your pain sits. For others, the actions of the storm that sit within you prevent you from being able to find forgiveness, and we say that both are real and both should be addressed.

We ask you here, what keeps you from forgiveness? Is it because something was stolen from you? A piece taken from you through that storm that occurred, that created that feeling within you? Or was it the actual storm? Was it the actual act? We say that here is something to think about, for it is important to understand where you sit as you wish to have forgiveness.

And we must say too that by not having forgiveness, how does that feel to you? How does not having forgiveness feel within you? How has not being able to forgive kept you from being your true self? How has not having forgiveness for that individual affected your relationships with other individuals?

What we wish to say to you here is that forgiveness should always be more about how you feel than the other person, you see. It is within you where the storm has created the damage, you see. It is within you that the storm of the words or the physical abuse, or the emotional abuse through the words, that these storms were created within you, you see.

Forgiveness is something that needs to come from within you as well. But it is important to understand why. Why forgiveness? How does forgiveness make you feel? How would forgiveness feel within you? How will forgiveness allow you to find those pieces that were taken in the storm? Do you see what we mean here?

Other people's behavior toward you, which we'll call the storm, came at you through physical contact, through emotional contact, through mental contact. These storms that have come to you through other individuals, it is those storms, the damage of those storms, you see, not the storm itself. For storms come in and out, you see.

We must look deeper at the repercussions of the storms. How have those storms within you affected you? Forgiveness sits within that answer, you see. When we have storms, storms come in, sometimes quite quickly, sometimes quite brutally, and sometimes with a vengeance. And as quickly as they come, they leave.

However, there are repercussions from those storms, you see. There are damages from those storms. And we say that within you, perhaps there has been damage. Where is your damage? Have the words affected you and how you see yourself? How has the damage affected you in your life? Has the damage prevented you from moving forward in life in the way you wish? Where does forgiveness sit with you?

It is important to know where the pain sits, you see, in order for the forgiveness to come. We must know where the pain is, where the damages of the storm sit, so we can go to the areas and begin to recover those areas. This is how we can then rebuild those areas, you see.

When you see the storms, the hurricanes, and the tornados coming through a city, you see great devastation. And when there is pain within you, there is devastation.

It is important to understand the degree of devastation that is sitting within you. One can only recover and rebuild when one can see and look deeper to where the damage is, you see. That is where we can forgive. Forgiveness is not possible until we can see where the damage is. Recovery isn't forgiveness, you see. Nevertheless, in order to forgive, we must recover.

We must know, within each of us individually, where the pain has sat. Where has the damage occurred in your life because of that storm? We say that when you can sit there a moment and feel that yes, it may be uncomfortable, as with those walking a hurricane site, tornado site, or an earthquake site where there has been great devastation.

It is very much the same within each who has endured great pain from someone. However, you see, it is possible to rebuild. You have seen in your life many cities that have been taken down by hurricanes and storms, and those cities have rebuilt.

But first they must walk the land, you see. Truly look at the land, at the devastation that was caused, and the degree of devastation that was caused. For you, it is the same, you see. It is very important to walk your own land and walk the land of that storm that transpired within you, feeling where the recovery is needed, and it is only then that forgiveness can occur.

Forgiveness can occur only once you begin to rebuild. However, you may not rebuild unless you walk the land so that you know what is needed to rebuild. Do you see what we mean? We say that many don't want to walk the land, many do not forgive, and they hang on with the land within them damaged from the storms that occurred through others' actions.

It is powerful for you to set the intention for yourself to put on your boots mentally and to begin walking the land of destruction that was caused within you through the storms of others. It is only then that you will be able to understand and know where the building and the rebuilding can occur, and when you do locate those areas, you see, forgiveness becomes easy. In that moment of rebuilding, you know you are stronger and that what you are building is stronger than what was there before, you see.

Sometimes walls come down and stronger walls can come up, and what we mean is that it is not for you to protect yourself. We say that through the experience we learn, you see. When those were built back in the day, there are now far newer ways of building today, you see, smarter ways of building today than perhaps once before.

We say it is the same with you, that with each storm, we learn, and through the pain, you learn your strength, you see. You uncover the builder that is within you. And that is very empowering, we say. It is quite empowering to uncover the builder that you are and to know that although your land and the structures within you have been taken down by the storms, that it is possible to rebuild.

As you walk the land that is within you and begin to take notice and pay attention and spend time understanding the feelings that you have, the feelings that were caused and given to you through these storms, you will also within you know ways of rebuilding, you see.

Only through the rebuilding process can forgiveness be found. Through the rebuilding process, you uncover yourself, you see, and you know within you what is possible for you. This is where you find forgiveness. It is far easier to find forgiveness for others when you know that within you, you are now stronger for it.

Therefore, we say that it will be quite nice for you to see yourself as a builder, you see, that you can rebuild from the storms that swept through you. Just as every hurricane site and every tornado site that you have seen on the television news, those lands are completely rebuilt anew in time, looking more beautiful and stronger than ever, you see.

Therefore, we say that forgiveness is a very powerful thing for you, you see. Forgiveness is about you; it is not for the other. Forgiveness allows you to clear up the storm, you see. Forgiveness allows you to clear up the storm, sweep up the debris and begin to build anew, and we say that this is quite beautiful.

We say for you to think of forgiveness this way and understand that forgiveness is always in your power. Forgiveness is always in your choosing. And we say that it is necessary if you wish to rebuild the land that is within you.

Moreover, it is important for us to say here that it is always possible, no matter the degree of the storm, no matter in what area within you the storm has affected or taken down, it is possible to rebuild it. To begin to forgive, it is only you walking through the land, through the debris that was caused from the storms that came at you, you see.

There is great value for you to walk that land and to clear that debris, and by doing so, there shall be a beautiful new day for you, better than before.

It is so. Until next time, there is great love for you here.

Edgar

Blooming through These Times of Change in Life

Indeed, it is again a nice time to be together in this way, for coming together in the way in which we are creates a lovely community. Would you agree?

We say it is a fine time in our world, even though some may not agree, for when change occurs in the world, there is uneasiness and unrest. We are each seeing this very much around at this time.

With each experience of uneasy and unrest will come more clarity, for the unease and the unrest truly is creating the clarity, you see. Among the world at this time, there are many who are feeling empowered, feeling a bit of a rumble within them, we say.

For many, this rumble within them gets them excited for this clarity. Within this clarity that is coming for the world in which you're in, there too is clarity within yourself, you see. It is very important to put focus there, for sometimes the uneasiness and the unrest that goes on around you there as new change is forming and creating a way to exist, you see. This change is creating its own form, and as it is forming and finding its shape, that within you too becomes new form, within the clarity that is being given to each of you. The clarity toward how you feel among what is happening. Clarity among the feelings in which you have in regard to the uneasiness, the unrest in the change that is surfacing around you. And for some of you, it's very uncomfortable, and we understand that change can be uncomfortable.

However, change, you see, is very important. It is necessary. It is mandatory, actually, for you cannot exist in the world in which you live without having change. It is not possible, you see. New things are always forming around you and with these new forms come new experiences, new ways of seeing things, a changed existence.

Within your world, if you can look back, many forms have taken shape. You see, if you look back, there is nothing that has ever stayed the same. And you are, yes, in a time now where great change is forming, taking shape, and finding its identity. And within you, you are finding your identity too, and we say this is quite good, don't you agree?

It is quite good to know that within you is change emerging as well, for you too can never be the same. You too are always changing, and experiences that showed up in your life—in the past, we say—have created great change for you. Experiences that have happened within you that have caused great pain have created great change with you as well.

Change is necessary—as we said, it's mandatory. Some of you are quite comfortable with change at a small level, while others of you are quite excited for big changes to occur and flow through.

Whether change is small or whether change is great, whether you are comfortable with change in small doses or change in a great dose, accept and understand and know that change is mandatory and change within you is mandatory as well.

Therefore, it is quite good for you to pay attention to the changes that are occurring within you and the changes that are occurring around you and the way you feel concerning the change that is happening ...

How do you feel about it? What sits uncomfortably for you? What sits and creates great excitement within you? There you will find much information about how you handle change and what type of change you resonate with you, for this is important to know as well.

Within each of you, there are changes that occur that you are more comfortable with than others, yes? And if you look back in your life experience, you will know and remember that certain changes were far harder to accept than others were.

Certain changes that occurred in your life were easier than others were. Moreover, you are in a time now in this world where change is necessary and mandatory, and it is also a time for you to take shape and change in how you view and see the changes that are occurring.

We are not here to tell you what is right for you and what is not right for you. We are here to tell you that it is time for you to make your own opinion upon that, and we are saying that it is only for us to tell you to sit within all the changes that are occurring and with the feelings of how it feels to you.

Are you one who is excited for the great change? Or are you one who is nervous about it? Are you one who can understand the mandatory occurrence of this change but uncomfortable with the magnitude in which it shows up?

Are you one who agrees with change but prefers it in small doses? Are you one who chooses to have great change in great ways instantaneously? You see, by knowing and understanding those questions, you will have great knowledge in to how you step in to change.

You are stepping in to change in the world in which you are in, for the world is changing around you; it is becoming anew, and we would prefer you to see this as a new bud ready to grow and open, to become.

Do you see change that way? Do you see change as a flower bud that has been wanting and waiting to be seen, to be heard, to be known? For this is truly where your world is at the moment—wanting expression. The flower bud is wanting to be expressed.

You could see change as a way to allow a bud to bloom. Realize that bud is you and enjoy the flower that it is becoming.

What we wish to say to you here is that there is great value for you to see change as positive. The comfort level at which change occurs for you is individual. How you choose to see the change that comes in the world is particular to each.

It is unique to each, and we say that is okay, that not all must jump onto change in the same way but know and understand that change is necessary; it is mandatory, and it is occurring, and it shall always occur.

So, as we said, see this change as a flower bud. It is for you to see yourself also as a flower bud. For when change occurs around you, it changes you. And as you look about the change that is occurring around you, it stirs something within you, and within that stirring, it creates change for you.

Can you see yourself as a flower bud also, wanting to bloom, wanting to understand the reasons that change is always so important? The world is constantly moving, energy is constantly moving in and out of things and people. Yes. Moving in and out of you.

Energy can never be still; it must always flow and go. And you too are energy, so you must flow and go as well. You are always a bud, needing to grow, to express itself, you see. That too is energy, and it's how you choose to see yourself, expressing yourself as it.

We say that it will be quite easy for you to sit with this just a little bit and feel into all these changes that are occurring in all the ways that they are. And to feel into which ones you're excited about and which ones you aren't.

Then ask yourself why you are excited for the ones that you are excited about and perhaps not about the others. What is it about some of the change that causes nervousness and uneasiness within you?

You see, by sitting and feeling into that, you water the bud that is you, and by watering the bud that is you, you begin to open yourself to opportunities that perhaps you weren't open to before. Open to the possibility of understanding things you didn't quite understand before.

As your bud opens, you bloom and as you bloom, you express, and as you are expressing, you are showing up in the world. And we say to you here, how do you wish to show up in the world?

What kind of flower are you? In what stage are you blooming? There is no wrong answer to what degree you are blooming. What we'd like to highlight here for you is that you are a bud and that you are blooming, and as you bloom, you grow, and through change, you grow as well.

Therefore, understand that circumstances, experiences, and change that are occurring all around you are allowing you to be that bud, to become that flower and to bloom. The more that you sit with that and pay attention to all the ways that these changes are affecting you—positively, negatively—how you are experiencing it in your life will tell you the degree of your blooming.

We wish to say to you that you are blooming, that these changes in the world are creating you to bloom, and we want you to know that. Whereas you can understand that a rose that is meant to bloom is most beautiful when it is blooming, when it opens.

When you go to the flower store to purchase a bouquet of roses, some of you might prefer the new roses that aren't quite open yet because you feel those will have more of a lasting effect. You will be able to enjoy them longer.

Others of you prefer that some of the flowers already be somewhat opened. And as those flowers open, they become quite beautiful, do they not? We wish for you to understand that you are a flower blooming in a time of much change and to know and understand that all the changes that are occurring around you, are for your blooming. We wish to express this to you here.

If you are a new bud or you are partially open, or you are wide open, as you are expressing yourself as that flower into the world, all is okay. It is only us here wanting to express to you that you, as the flower, are blooming as well. This means that you too are changing. Moreover, through the energy of the world, which is showing up here, it is creating change within you and it is for you to understand that change is a positive thing. Even if it is an uncomfortable change, it is necessary for you to bloom.

Therefore, we wish so much for you to see yourself this way. Sit a moment and say in your blooming process, here, now, with all that is occurring around the world, "How have I shown up? How am I experiencing this? How is it changing me? How am I growing through it? Where am I in the blooming process?" This shall tell you quite a lot.

We wish to say to you as well that you are each beautiful, and whether you see all that is going on as uncomfortable for you and perhaps not agreeing with all of it, or agreeing with all of it, we say it is all okay.

It is information for you to understand where your work lies, where your understanding sits, where your comfort level is. And there in itself, by just becoming aware of that, it is allowing you to grow and is allowing your bud to bloom and grow right where you are, but know that you are and know that the experiences that life is presenting are helping you to do that.

That is what we wish you to know. Ponder this a bit, understand this a bit, and we say that we very much like these times together working this way. We love coming forward to be of value to you in the way in which we can.

We come forward here today with great love, all with wanting you to see the beautiful flower that you are and the continuous blooming that you are doing, and we wish for you to see yourself this way as well.

It is so. Until next time, there is great love for you here.

Edgar

Finding Peace within, Being in the Moment

Indeed. As we say many times as we step in this way, it is in fact a lovely way to be, and we say for you each being there where you are that it too is a lovely way to be. Do you see it? More importantly, do you feel it? Do you feel that you, where you are, the way you are, is in fact a lovely way to be?

There can be great joy in allowing yourself to just feel in the moment how you are in life, as we are in this moment, coming forward this way, feeling into the way we are here, coming forward for you in this way. Indeed, it is a lovely way to be.

We wish to speak a bit about being and all the different ways that you can be in your life. Sitting here listening to us or reading this on the pages is a way to be. When you sit and you are in this way, what is your intention? It is to settle in, is it not? Come to listen. Come to experience the words we have for you today.

There is joy within you when you do this, yes? The wanting to gather, the wanting to be, the wanting to listen, to settle in and to hear the words that are expressed for you. And we say in life that it is very much the same, but do you settle into your life in the way that you settle in here at this moment, allowing yourself to be, allowing yourself to settle into what life has for you, or are you always running through life, not allowing life to give you what it is possible for you to receive?

What we wish to say to you here is that there is great value in being in the present moment, giving to yourself and allowing yourself to just be. This is in fact giving of yourself, giving to yourself, giving for yourself, you see. But do you do it?

We say right now, right here, absorbing these words, you are. But do you make a habit of doing this? Do you make a habit of making time for yourself? To be for yourself? This is one way to be. However, there are many ways that you can do that for yourself. Do you?

We ask you what you would like to do for yourself? Feel. Feel what that would be. What are those experiences that you would like to have? What are those moments that you would like to feel?

What are those things that you can make yourself available for and don't? Is there value sitting with your cup of coffee? Or your tea? Or your cocoa? Is there value in holding that mug, just sitting and being?

We say there is. Is there a value for you to spend that ten minutes prior to getting out of bed and just sit and be with yourself there, lying in the bed? Do you do that? Or do you jump out of bed? And as you jump out of bed, if you are who one that does that, do you find your life a bit hectic? Can you see that there is value in awakening to start your day and just lying in your bed a moment longer before putting your feet upon the floor? We say there is.

Do you look out your window and is your attention drawn to things outside your window? Do you place a moment there with what it is that draws your attention and just settle with that for a moment or two?

We say that there's great value for you if you do. So many are always looking to keep themselves busy, so many running from one section of the day to another. What we wish to say to you here is that there is indeed such great value in just slowing yourself down a bit, for as you slow yourself down a bit, you slow your mind down a bit as well, you see.

That mind of yours is what gets you going quickly. However, you can learn to practice a bit here in your day and just be a little bit more with yourself, whether it be three minutes, five minutes, ten minutes. It matters not the degree of time, just that you make the time, you see.

You learn to practice, creating this space for yourself, learning through the day of allowing this to be, you see. When you stop and eat lunch, do you choose to eat your lunch with your device in your hands, checking your emails, your messages, your media, your voice mails? Or do you allow yourself to just sit and be with yourself and the food, paying attention to the chewing of your food, listening to the liquid that enters your body, and do you take a moment to feel that liquid entering and going through your body?

Do you pay attention to the number of times that you chew? Are you one who eats quickly? Are you one who likes to be active and busy as you are eating? We say that there is great value in taking that moment to just be with the meal, to be with the food, to be with yourself with the food—just you and it.

We say that there is great value in do that. If you are one who takes a walk, do you take a walk and talk on the telephone? Or do you allow yourself to be with the walk and take in the experiences of the walk? The experiences life has given you for that walk? Or are you walking past it, putting focus and attention into activity, opposed to what life is showing you, what nature is showing you? We say that there is great value for you to slow it down and do activities that bring yourself there—and just yourself—leaving the external things to the side.

What we wish to say to you here is that many of you find it uncomfortable and uneasy just to allow yourself these few moments just to be with yourself. We say that it would be very nice for you each to maybe try things a little differently. When you are in the kitchen and you are cooking a meal and you have something in the pan sizzling, become aware of yourself and of this pan and allow the sound of the sizzling to affect you. It can, if you allow it.

Or is your mind going in different places as you are cooking with that pan? There are many ways in a day, in the things that you do, that would be lovely for you to leave everything aside and just be with yourself for

143

those moments. As you listen to the sizzling and you bring yourself to the sizzling, listen and hear the sizzling; it does create something within you, for in that moment, you are with that sound only. When you eat and you are just with the food, you and itself are there, allowing yourself to have that experience, you see, with no external factors present with you but you and that food. And that is allowing you a moment to be with yourself, you see.

All of these moments that we speak of, whether it be sitting with that coffee in your hand and enjoying that, whether it be spending a few moments in your bed prior to putting your feet upon the ground, whether it be walking within nature and allowing yourself no phone calls or music whatsoever, just being, allow you to be with yourself.

There are many ways to pause and be with yourself. And these are all wonderful training exercises, you see, and we call them training exercises because these are little ways for you to learn to practice, to settle in and be with yourself a little bit.

There is no need to have to do this in big ways. There are wonderful opportunities within your day to spend in little ways to just settle in and be with yourself. It doesn't need to be much time. It could be three minutes; it could be five minutes. It could be just enjoying that cup of coffee or those few extra moments of just being with yourself, awake, lying in bed before you put your feet on the ground. And what we say to you is that this is wonderful for you, for all of these ways allows you to recharge yourself, you see.

Many of you run with a battery that is running low, and these are wonderful, easy ways for you to plug in and recharge, you see? If you try, you will find that you will enjoy, and as you try, you do, and as you enjoy, you will find more ways you see within your day where you can pause for just a few moments and enjoy these things and be just with you. Know that this is giving to yourself and that these are easy ways to do it.

Therefore, we leave you here with some things to ponder, ways that you can be with yourself in your day, easy ways that you can do it. There are more, and it is for you to find within your day those ways that are more. It is the starting point for you, you see. And we just wish to give you something that you most likely do already, but maybe you can find a way to do it with a little bit more stillness, we say.

We say to set the intention of finding these little easy ways and to make it for you to be quiet and to know that this is recharging yourself. We come forward always to give you easy ways to add upon your day a way to recharge you, to feel yourself, and to experience the peace within you, for there is great peace within you, and it is only sitting truly with yourself that you shall find it. There are lovely ways within your day that you can do that. We say to do that.

It is so. Until next time, there is great love for you here.

Edgar

A Path and Road in Life

Good morning Edgar,

What letter do you want to write today for Letters from Spirit? What do you wish to share or teach us?

Yes, indeed a lovely time to sit, to be with you each here and to discuss, to discuss any topic of interest we like to express for you. There is indeed so much to be shared and talked about. You each may have much you want to hear.

It is so.

We say today we wish to speak of your road and your path in your life. Where you get on it and where it takes you. Many here want to be directed, guided towards the path that is right for you. We understand, we see the importance you feel in wanting to be on this path in life that is for you.

Many here feel they are not on any path or road at all in life that is taking them anywhere. Many of you feel stuck. You feel a bit frustrated as you want to get going, but unsure of where to go. No road or path has shown up for you. Would you agree?

We say here that the paths in your life are many and we wish you to understand that there is never not a path for you. Many of you stop in life and look around you and see none and we say, oh yes, they are there.

Many paths, so how do you locate yours? How can you become aware of a path and know it is for you?

We say paths that take you in and through life are always forming and building. We wish you to imagine a road being created, you see, on your streets. You have seen this yes? Roads being paved. You see the trucks and workers, laying down the concrete, smoothing the road and creating the lines for the lanes to help you each with which is the right side and which is the wrong side.

We say here this is a good visual for you for as you can see how roads in your cities are built, it is very much the same for you.

In life you may go through difficult times, this is your path being dug up. You may go through times in life where you feel uncertain of yourself because of events that had occurred, and we say this too is the road being paved for you.

Through creating and making roads, you have at times a bit of a mess. It can be frustrating with traffic backed up and you smell the tar from the forming of the new streets. We say new streets as that is what is being laid for the betterment of those vehicles on the roads, yes? Smoother, better driving roads to take you each to your destination.

This process creates a bit of inconvenience and even annoyance as the roads are being laid. In your life you may have had a change happen in life that now asks of you what now? Where do I go? Where do I head now?

Those difficult times or events are your roads being paved; you see.

It is life acting as your construction worker, creating new for you. It is you getting repaved you see. Once the road is complete, your travel down it is far more enjoyable than before, when the road was filled with potholes and ditches.

Do you agree? In fact, a brand-new road has been created that was never there and now it is and you can enjoy a better driving experience. The new road in your city created a way for less traffic, more efficiency and easier access to other roads.

Your life will have many roads under construction or under repair. Construction and repair is for improvement and will always be. When you are going through challenges, it is life giving you improvements, but during this process you must have a bit of mess first you see.

We wish to give you another visual to consider here, about your path and how it looks, so you can know you have placed yourself on the right one.

We say it is shaped as a smile. Your road that is right for you is designed and shaped as a smile on your face. This is the perfectly paved, redesigned and perfectly repaired road. That is your road.

To know you are on the path that takes you in a good direction is simply to know you are smiling. The smile, along with the feeling that made you smile, is always your traffic light to say go, move forward and put your foot on the accelerator. Go this direction, your path is here.

The smile tells you what the right path is, and your feeling of the smile lets you know where the road leads you. Be aware of your road showing up upon your face and where it is wanting to lead you through how the smile makes you feel. This is your map. Your decision to act upon it is your foot on the pedal going through the traffic light.

It is so. Until next time, there is great love for you here.

Edgar

Detours in Life

Good morning Edgar,

I sit today to prepare the next Letters from Spirit for those tuning in. What do you have to say to all of us? What do you want to share for us?

Indeed, it is a fine time. It is you at this moment who is not feeling as fine. We say today would be good to touch upon what you are feeling because as we feel, others feel the same.

We wish to discuss detours in life. What are they? Why do they occur in the lives of many?

It is that you each have experienced times in life where things did not work out for you the way you had expected, times in your life where you went down a road that was not in the direction you had planned for your life.

In times in your life you have each been on the road driving down what we shall call The Life Road. This Life Road brings you through many streets on your journey. It is filled with different experiences, different landscapes, different views.

These roads are your life path. Paths switch, change and often the place you are wanting to go is not yet ready for you. It is needing more work from you before heading down that road. So you end up in a detour, a road that takes you on a bit of an extended journey to your headed destination.

Do you understand here what we try to say? It is that where you are wanting to be in your life and the direction you must go to get there is and will always have more than one direct route. When you are charted down a new course you feel it to be a roadblock, because the direction is not what you had chosen to go or imagined, so you feel defeated and frustrated.

This switching of direction now changes the vibration frequency in you by the response you gave to it. This shift in vibration alters the direction of your destination. It is not that where you were planning was wrong, for if it was a feeling you had that gave you inspiration or excitement or visions of what you want, then it is not the wrong destination.

We say though the route you were wanting to take yourself down to get there is what was not correct, so life then must reroute you. This gets many feeling that what they want cannot be, that what they want cannot come to fruition, to see, feel, have and touch it.

We say this is never the case. It is your own vibration that takes you off of the detour and away into the woods with no road at all in a space that does not feel good to you.

We say allow. We say allow the detours.

Have you driven your vehicle heading someplace and you found a detour sign that led you off the road you were driving on? Wanting to head onto a highway but found it to be closed and you are redirected to the next one?

Have you ended up on a journey with your navigation directing you off the road you thought you should be on? Taking you down and through streets and cities unexpectedly? Do you know why that is?

It is to avoid something. It can be an accident. It can be traffic. It can be road construction. It can be a water pipe burst or fires that now need streets closed. It can be many reasons why you were re-navigated on that day.

When you got rerouted, did you eventually end at your destination? We say you did. Why is it then in your life that you do not trust your own life navigation?

If you can all see that these detours that show up in your life are not to prevent you from arriving exactly where you wish to be in life, it is only showing you new roads to take. On these roads you may be shown new things.

The new route allows perhaps time for what you wish to be, have or do to catch up to you. Detours in life are always there to realign you to a better journey, one that when you do arrive to, it is now ready for you.

Sometimes you must slow it down and catch your breath a bit, dear ones. Trust is very important when you travel through life. If you can move along in life with the knowing and understanding that detours are not roadblocks for you, that when you are now heading a different way to get where you wish to be, know and understand that this is life preparing the road for you and to trust it is for you and not against you.

We are sure here you can have a memory within you that you can remember a time where you were heading somewhere, you got detoured and the new roads you were directed to was a fine drive indeed and that you did arrive at your destination.

Isn't this most important, that you arrived? If it was of a different time, know it became the perfect time for you to show up to it.

Go along your life journey knowing and understanding that with all the roads you will travel down, there will be some detours. You will be redirected from time to time to go in a new direction, but you still arrive. We want you to know this as the understanding will help you with the trust we spoke of earlier you see.

We say take the journey through life with an open heart. Open to the changes of the landscape and know the roads you get redirected to is part of your journey. Smile and hold trust, we say, as you head down it with excitement of what is waiting for you. With the new roads often comes something extra for you when you do arrive.

It is so. Until next time, there is great love for you here.

Edgar

Why your story is important

illlllllllllllllllllllllllllllllllllllllllllllllllllllllllllllllllllllllllllllllllllllllllllllllllllllllll

Good morning Edgar,

What shall be discussed today for our Letters from Spirit? What would you like to share?

Good morning indeed. It is indeed a good morning. We say to be here to step forward is always something we enjoy doing. It is so.

You ask the question, what shall we share? Yes, share is a good word, for within it are many good feelings and outcomes. We coming in this way is us sharing ways for you each to see yourselves and your lives in new fresh ways, and this very much is us expressing joy through the act of sharing.

It is so.

Sharing is something each of you can do as well. In one way or another you are all sharing. Sharing is a way of giving. It is a gesture of giving. Giving, we say, is always very nice. To share and to give can show up in many ways. Each of you here listening now have very much that can be shared with others.

Do you know this?

We say you all have something to share. You all have within you a story to share. Today we wish to speak of your story. Do you know yours? Have you spent time understanding the importance of your story? Do you know your story is created to be shared, whether it be in big ways or in small ways? Stories are a way of giving. It too is a way to heal, to heal others and to heal yourself during the act of it.

What can you share from your life story?

Your story has so much that allows expression to occur for another. It is never for you to just hold it within you. That would be like a seed never getting the opportunity to bloom into its possibility. It is the beauty of living these stories and sharing the stories that create so much for the world. It is the seeds that became the beautiful flowers.

Can you see your story as something worth sharing? When you share stories it is like you are giving flowers to another.

Stop a moment and feel into a chapter of your life. This may be a chapter you found great success in, perhaps it is a career. You feel into the how's and the what's you did to achieve your success story.

Can you see that how you achieved it gives you great experience and this can be shared? Do you think that someone can be moved by your story and hearing it from you moves them positively to try for themselves something they have wanted to do? Do you know that your story can motivate another to want to take action?

Have you gone through tremendous loss? Loss of a loved one now with spirit once more? Has that pain in your heart felt overwhelming? Has it brought you to your knees in some of the pages of your story? Has the pain gotten you to pray?

Has it questioned your own mortality? Has the loss softened you? Has the loss given you new faith? Have you gone through the many different emotions, through the pain of loss and if so can you see your steps through those emotions was a way to walk yourself slowly out from the deepest part of your pain?

Can you see that this pain has given you ways of finding yourself a bit different and changed from it? Could you see that through this experience you can understand loss in a way you once could not? Knowing that what the experience has taught you about the steps of grief and what you have learned from it, can be shared with another who is now beginning those emotional steps themselves, experiencing the same as you once did at the start of yours?

Can sharing your story of your steps forward through the emotions be of help to another who has not stepped as far as you? Can your sharing of your pain heal another and still heal you?

We say it can and will.

Have you ended a relationship through divorce or separation, once depending on another and now needing to depend on yourself? Have you learned your strengths through this time? Through depending on yourself, has it taught you more about you and the resilience you have within you? Finding your way through the changes and by doing so finding a new you?

What have you learned about yourself? What did you find out about you? Do you see yourself stronger, more capable than you once believed? Was there a time you felt your world was over and now you see yourself in it much differently?

Did you find your smile again, with more hope now? Why? What steps did you take to take yourself from feeling all alone to perhaps enjoying a bit of the alone time? Feeling you did not know yourself truly outside of that relationship but now you see a stronger version of yourself?

Are you learning to love yourself? Do you think you can share your story about finding your courage and finding your strength within?

We say you can.

You see dear ones, these are examples for you. There are many chapters to your life story and there are happy chapters and not so happy chapters. It is that through the chapters that are not so happy that the learning, the growing and the discovery comes for you.

As you step through the pages of those chapters, you step towards the section of your life story with a new sense of self and to another new, happier chapter once more.

The chapters in your life will have both happy and not so happy moments, and there is indeed a place of sharing that can come from each. You each have ways to give back, to share, to know that each moment in your life is giving you an opportunity to share, to be a part of something greater, something that can be of great importance.

For each of your chapters are important and each of your following chapters are also important and your life comes with very much importance for others you see.

Do you know this?

We say what chapter would you like to share? With which pages would you like to highlight and give to others as a way to make your difference to the world? This is a way to be of service.

Whether it be the pages or the chapter or the entire story you wish to share, it all has purpose for you and will touch another. How your life was, how it changed, and how it changed you and where you stand now because of it.

Where are your highlights in your story? We say highlights to mean where have you found the change in you that can make a change in another? What can you share where your strength came from in times of great sorrow or hardship? How are you rebounding? What steps did you do to rebound or what steps are you taking now towards your comeback story?

It is too, a very good chapter in your story when you are able to share the preparation and your steps of your comeback. The honesty in sharing your moments of your falls and the perseverance you found within of getting back up once again.

Can you see how important you are? All that you have to share? The difference you make?

We say begin writing your story. It is not something that must be on a shelf in a virtual bookstore or other store. It is not something that must be spoken in front of big audiences. It can be shared any way you feel comfortable and we say there are so many ways to tell your story and to share your experiences of your recovery from hardship to success, from sadness to joy, from insecurity to confidence, through your heartache and the healing and through the moments you are in currently. Even if you are not quite through a chapter yet.

There is much to share regarding the steps forward you are making. Through sharing your story, you too are making more steps forward for yourself as well.

This is very good indeed.

We wish to say that you each have stories and stories are always to be shared. Sharing is giving. Sharing life experiences offers the greatest gift.

So feel your story, feel into your pages, feel into the chapters you have already completed and the one you are still writing, and see yourself as one who is here to share it. It shall create great positive movement within you and too within others.

You are important and this is your important work.

It is so. Until next time, there is great love for you here.

Edgar

The Artist

||||||||||||||||||||||||||||||||||||||||||||||||||||||||||||||||||||||||||||||||||||||||||||||||||||||||||||||||||||||||||||||||||||||||||||||||||||||||

Good morning Edgar,

I would like to write together today a new letter for our Monday Letters from Spirit. What can we share? What can be spoken to help someone forward?

Yes, a good day to you. It is always that we can be available to those that sit to hear our guidance.

We wish to speak of possibilities. We feel that there are many out there sitting by the windowsill looking out and not actively participating, not feeling possibilities. We say that much has moved within the energy of your world that has kept so many in their chairs.

We say to sit is not something that is wrong to do, but we say as well if it is sitting that continues for long periods we see that many forget to walk again. What we mean to say here is the desire to go has become less, the desire to move less. We say action must be within oneself to create. Yes, you can sit and still have action like an artist who paints. This can be a good example.

An artist can sit for many hours and paint. The artist paints what is being expressed from within themselves. They are taking action. They feel within them and it goes onto the canvas. This is action.

An artist can sit for many days doing this. They are, however, moving with inspiration are they not? They may be sitting, they may be quiet, they may do it for days. They are however creating from the expression of what is being felt within them. They are taking action. From the action they create.

161

The paint expresses their inner feelings. What they paint may be different each time they sit, but they are creating onto the canvas.

We say many are sitting, looking through the windows of their life and not painting. Not expressing. When there is too much sitting with no action towards something, you then can feel a bit confused about where you are in your life.

Nothing makes sense to you on how to express, what to express or even wanting to express. We say it is important to express. It is good for you to express and to move with it.

Can you become a painter? You must not need to be an artist, for some think an artist is not possibly within them. We say paint. Painting as you look out the windows of your life, can you see areas you wish to go? Can you look out your windows and wish to see something else?

As a painter or artist, you can begin to hold the brush in your hand and begin. Begin creating. Take action towards what you wish to see from your windows, what you wish to see for you.

Do you know what you want? We say you do. Perhaps not always completely, but you do know. We say to begin creating looking out the window is a wonderful thing to do, but it is only one part of your creating process.

You must sit and feel and then you must allow the feelings from your desires to become the paint. As you paint, what is the feeling morphing into? What is your hand painting?

We use painting as a way to understand that you can create from how you feel. We say you do create from how you feel. You are painters and artists. You are indeed. It is a wonderful exercise for you to practice a bit, perhaps with an activity of actual painting.

Have you done this? Have you sat and simply painted? You will be surprised by what will show up on your canvas.

It feels good to be an intentional creator. Many are creating not intentionally. Many create by default. In fact, many are creating art without the understanding that they are in fact creating images onto their life canvas.

When you can place intention towards your creative process, you will see a landscape painted upon your canvas that is of your liking. It is then that you can look out your window of life and see the scenery that is of your wanting.

Have you lived with paintings in your life you do not like, you do not get pleasure from, you do not resonate with? One can just simply change the art on the walls in their life and begin to create the art they find more joy from.

What is that for you? This is when the sitting at the window is an important part of any creative process. But we ask you here now, are you sitting with images in your mind of the art you have lived with upon your personal walls that you no longer like or perhaps never did, or are you sitting by the window and designing within you what you prefer to have hanging up on those walls of yours now?

Can you see that you are painting them? Your thoughts, your desires, your feelings, your intent. Many times we see much art hanging on the walls of lives of others that was never intended to be hung, but many hung them up anyway. This is creating art by default and not with intent.

You are each your own artist. To paint is to express. To move with your desires is creating. To simply sit in the chair with your mind always focused on the painting you do not like simply creates for you more copies of the same.

We say take down the paintings you do not like and stop focusing on them. If the walls are bare a bit understand you are just in the process of designing and creating a beautiful art piece for your life that will become your new window to look out through and enjoy with far better views and experiences.

It is so. Until next time, there is great love for you here.

Edgar

The Gift of You

Good morning Edgar,

I am happy to sit with you and work in this way. What would you like to share with us?

Nice indeed, we say. It is a wonderful time when we can all gather together in this most wonderful way, allowing you each here to uncover the wonderful way you each are.

It is so. You ask what shall we share?

We say sharing is a nice word and a great act of doing. Would you agree? Many of you carry within you a wonderful gift. For some of you, you are aware of these gifts. For others you are not. We say you each have gifts to share and give to the world that is around you.

We say this is a beautiful way to be, to give, to share and to express the gifts within you.

Many of you who are unaware of these divine gifts that have been specifically placed within you say, how do I know my gifts? How do I uncover my gifts? How can I know they are there? Why do I not know of them? If they are within me I would know this.

We say a gift within you is to be opened. A gift within you needs to be unwrapped, we say. Think of yourselves as a beautifully wrapped present. What is inside that package?

You hold a gift in your hands and you are filled with excitement, you see. What is in this special package given to me? Do you feel this way about yourself? Do you see yourself as a beautiful gift given to the world?

You do not.

It is a time now for you each to see yourselves as a magnificent package, a beautifully wrapped gift. It is within you. It is for you to open to see what is inside. Do you see here what we mean?

You do not go about life seeing yourself as a marvelous gift to the world, perfectly wrapped, specifically for you to express. You see, dear ones, it is this gift of self that has within it qualities. You have qualities that are wonderfully specific to you. Yes you. Do you wish to open them? Do you wish to receive the gift that has been placed within you, for you to have and share?

We say it is time. You ask us how, how does one find that beautiful gift within? We say you must first know and believe that it is there. You see so many do not have faith in themselves. We wish you to have faith and belief in yourself. It is that you must feel that indeed the gift is within you and it takes only you to recognize it and then wanting to receive it.

Is it that you perhaps do not feel that you are deserving of gifts? Are you feeling that a gift within you, so important that it can be shared with the world, is even possible?

We say here lays the very issue. We say you must understand the gift within self, you must first recognize that you are indeed a gift. Do you? Do you see yourself as someone who has something to share, to give?

You do. You all do. To know what is inside your precious, beautiful package you must only have the excitement of seeing this in yourself and wanting to know, having the curiosity to open it. You see with curiosity and excitement very much unfolds. So many of you go through life with the feeling of "this is what I am" and "this is what I do" and "this is all I have" and we say no, there is far more, so much more.

You have many gifts, begin to want to see them. Begin to build the desire of wanting to know what is in that package that is you. You must want to know. Do you? Ask yourself. With desire and curiosity you open the package you see.

You must understand this. To have desire towards anything creates it to be. To have a desire to know your gifts is the unwrapping of them. We say life is imagination, you see. There must be play within your hearts.

Is there? Do you have play in your heart? When you receive a gift how does that feel?

Pause a moment here now and feel. Close your eyes and remember when a beautifully wrapped gift was given to you. When was this? Who was it from? How did you feel in your heart? Feel.

Was there excitement fluttering through you? Were you excited to receive something? Was there curiosity running within you of wondering what was inside? Was it packaged in a way that gave you joy within? As you opened it, how did you feel? Were you happy to receive?

We say yes you were. Open your eyes now. Breathe.

Now with your eyes closed once more - see yourself as the gift. Imagine you as a beautiful wrapped gift. Do you feel the same way now as you did just a moment ago? Do you have excitement flushing through you, curiosity running about you? Is there a wanting to receive? Excited for what is inside?

For so many we say no, you do not have this excitement.

We wish you each to know whether in this moment you can understand this or not, you are a beautiful gift to the world. You have great importance in being here in this time, place and space. You have within you gifts! You have ways to share it.

Are you? Do you? If you answer no, then we say your faith of who you are is a bit low. We say get excited. See yourself as we see you all. Believe you have great worth within you, always wishing to be expressed. Indeed, you each do. You have gifts that when shared give joy, you see.

To unwrap your gifts, simply become excited about opening them. We say this builds desire and desire unwraps your gifts. Do you see?

We wish here to step forward and to just allow you the opportunity to see yourself a new way. The right way. You are each a magnificent gift to the world and each have something to share and you must want to know what they are, and once you do you must become excited for the unveiling of it, you see. With excitement comes curiosity and desire and this is unwrapping your gifts.

We say open your package. It is not meant to stay wrapped. It is meant to be opened, shared and enjoyed, and as you become aware so too will your way of sharing and expressing the gift of you to your world you see. This we say will give much joy to you and many.

It is so. Until next time, there is great love for you here.

Edgar

What's on your Calendar?

Good morning Edgar,

What do you wish to share for this upcoming Letters from Spirit?

Indeed. We smile here now as we are given this opportunity to once again be with you and to be here with all joining in for our guidance, our teachings, our way to shine light towards your wellness.

We say today we wish to touch upon the topic of calendars. Yes, calendars. Some of you now may wonder what we can say towards something so simple. Something that you all are already understanding.

Are you using this calendar that you live by properly?

Calendars are there to help you remember appointments, to keep you organized and to help you arrange your days, your weeks in your life. So many of you filling up the days and weeks with many things, and others with no things at all.

If you now could open your calendars, what would you find? What would you see your coming week becoming for you?

Are there activities placed within the days of things that give you joy? Are you looking at things you have put upon your calendar and feel excited about that day arriving into your experience? Is there anything placed onto your calendar that is specifically for you?

We do not mean doctor's appointments. We do not mean dentist appointments. We mean a time blocked out in your calendar for your personal wellness. For enjoyment. For pleasure. For peace. Is this on your calendar?

We see you each being very good towards the doing each week of all of your responsibilities. You have many and we understand the need to do them. Filling your appointments up with what needs to get done, what must get taken care of, priorities, we say.

We say the biggest priority must always be about you. Do you forget that very important priority? Is that responsibility to yourself on your schedule?

Perhaps for a few of you, a small percentage. We would very much like that percentage to rise much higher.

Why? Why are you filling your days and weeks with only time for responsibility outside of yourself and no play for your inner wellness? We have spoken in previous letters regarding the importance of play.

Do you do it?

We ask you to now ask yourself this question. Why do I not put play into my schedule? Why do I place play in my schedule for others, but not me? Why is the responsibility of my inner joy not accounted for in my daily or weekly appointments? Why do I not give myself the wellness appointment regularly?

Why?

What holds you away from giving yourself the time? We say you have all become very trained in utilizing and making a calendar for getting your things done, getting things handled, getting things accomplished.

We ask you why you do not see your happiness as wellness and see the need for this to be necessary to get it done, to get it accomplished and to get it handled. These should be your priorities as well.

Are you handling your happiness? Are you making happiness a priority? Look at your calendar. It will tell you your own answer.

Many say I am too tired at the end of a day to do anything for me. We say then start your day with yourself at the morning appointment when you are not tired.

Some say I have nothing I feel desire towards doing, so I do nothing. We say then schedule time for yourself to be the one to seek. To seek things to find desire in. Make the appointment to discover.

Name one hour "The Discovery Hour". Here you can allow yourself time to play with ideas. Look up vision boards others have created for their happiness. Do you see anything you like or would enjoy on the boards of others? Have you looked?

Can you create a happiness vision board for yourself? We say you can. This is yet another appointment in the week that can be added, a fun one as well. Seek and you shall find. Seek images that give you a happy stir within and transfer that image to your happy board. We very much enjoy visions, for it is a way for you to see and from the seeing you can have an emotion about it. This emotion stirs up the desires and this is how you may find more interests, and this will create a wanting within to do them.

We wish you to look at your calendars with a new set of eyes. With the eyes of wellness. Create time each day or each week towards your wellness. We say it is very easy to get off the road of wellness when you follow a road that is titled "My to do list" or "My calendar" and there is nothing on either leading you to wellness for you.

It is time to make yourself a better facilitator of your daily happiness. It is you, after all, who is in charge of your calendar and no one else. You hold the pen. You hold the day in your hands and you also hold the calendar in your hands as well.

It is time now to begin filling a week with more fun, with more things to get you excited. More things, we say, that allow you to be caring of your own wellbeing. This can be in simple tasks. This must not ever need to be hard tasks. It is only hard when you become too far removed from the idea of wellness and you do not gift yourself the time to have it.

We say having it is a very good idea. It should always be on your to do list.

We say get going towards creating new calendars for yourself, a calendar for your wellness. Add in what feels good and is for you and remove or space out a bit the things that are your burdens.

By creating more time for yourself, you may look towards those burdens and responsibilities with fresher, newer eyes and see them as far more doable now that better balance has been created in your daily and weekly life.

We come today to say it is ok that you, until today perhaps, have had nothing in your calendar for your happiness. It is that now you understand more and from this understanding you will create more, more for you and we are very much looking forward to seeing that.

It is so. Until next time, there is great love for you here.

Edgar

The Light Show

||||||||||||||||||||||||||||||||||||||||||||||||||||||||||||||||||||||||||||||||||||||||||||||||||||||||||||||||||||||||||||||||||||||||||||||||||||||||

Good morning Edgar,

I sit to receive a new letter for our Letters from Spirit. What shall the topic be today? What do you wish to speak about?

It is a good day when we can be together this way, to create a collaboration of our efforts together to serve others.

It is a good day indeed.

We say we can speak of many topics, but all topics should be focused on the self. We say all that we speak of is to be for the self. To allow you all who join in to better know your significance to the world in which you live in.

It is that you all carry within you a light. It is a light that can intensify from hour to hour, lighter or brighter and too it can weaken from the hour before as well. It is that you each carry this inner light within you and your controller of this light and the strength of it lays within your own feelings. It is too that your feelings control how the light is amplified.

Your light wishes to be expressed within your day, you see. It is that within you, you hold great power, and it is that light within you that carries that power. You see dear ones, you are a bit of a walking glow stick. You are always beaming light from yourself. It is how we each here see you.

It is so.

Your feelings and emotions trigger the switch of your inner light and cast the degree of light that is expressed from you. The brighter the light that is expressed, the happier it is you are feeling. You know and understand what a happy thought feels like. You know and understand what a happy emotion feels like. You have each expressed it in your life. That is when your light is illuminating in the way it is intended.

Do you know and understand the effect of your light? Can you understand why your light is important to another? It is, if we can say in the simplest of terms, no different than your city. Have you witnessed your city with all the lights shining and all the lights on?

You can understand that the light affects the city and gives an experience that is much more enjoyable than when the city has no lights on at all.

Can you imagine the city of Las Vegas with no lights shining? What would that experience be like for all of those walking the streets? We say you are each very much like that. Your light illuminating outward from you onto your own streets. You affect the streets and those that are walking on them every day.

Let us give you a smile as an example here.

When you smile, it turns on your power beam. It allows your inner light to shine. It creates rays of light that seep out of you and onto the streets and into another to feel. A smile is created from a feeling, from a thought, from an emotion. Each smile creates a ray of light that gets expressed. As you walk the streets in your town or village, you are giving out light beams just as the lights do in Las Vegas, you see.

You must understand that your wattage of power within you is greater than the wattages of the city of Las Vegas.

It is so.

For the positive feelings and thoughts give out powerful wattages of light beams that carry far further in energy than the lights of the city we mention here.

You see, your energy when created with the power of your emotions, can affect and light up all that is around you and beyond what you cannot see. Your smile can be felt farther than the light of a city, you have that much wattage within you.

Your light travels because of your power.

How do you amplify the wattage to the degree it touches those that are not even in your city? We say by intentions. To merely intend to step into your day with your light on and not off. The city of Las Vegas looks far different when the lights are not on. Do you agree?

It is the same with you when you carry within you emotions and feelings that keep your wattage low. It will not give you the experiences you seek.

With low wattage there is no power to illuminate the skies. We say your power sits within the intentions to have joy.

We say a smile can carry on for miles, you see. It has a chain reaction. One smile given to another creates another smile which creates within them a new, better feeling which then powers up their wattage, you see. You are all the lights of a great city with an impressive landscape.

As Las Vegas is meant to beam up, so too are each of you. You are meant to shine brilliantly. You are meant to light up the world. You are all a piece of light that together shines upon each other to create light within another. A light show you see.

Each of you servicing one another's power source within so it may illuminate, each recharging another so there is never the possibility of a power outage. We say to have feelings and emotions that create the smile upon your face, which illuminates you and as another sees it, it illuminates them, you see, and as that smile allows another to feel good, it is those feelings that create the next smile that is then shared to another.

You see, as we said, a chain reaction.

This is how we keep all the lights on, beaming beautifully onto each other and then all are surrounded by the magnificence of the lights. It will be indeed felt everywhere. You are all a part of this light show. It is not to be any other way.

We say for some of you it has been difficult to keep your lights on and bright. We come here today to express to you the beautiful light that you offer to the world. Each light reflects from another and together you create a world that is bright within you, you see.

We say to think happy thoughts and know as you do, the light within you brightens. Build upon the emotions that give joy to you as this is strengthening your wattage and know that you are a powerful source of light to the world. Your light is needed to shine and needed to help the world become bright once again.

It is so. Until next time, there is great love for you here.

Edgar

Are You Sitting on the Sidelines in Life?

Indeed. We are always happy to step forward and work in this way—to be here and share thoughts. To get you thinking, you see. And more importantly, to get you feeling. For life gives you many things to feel. Life truly is a playground of feelings. It is your playground to feel. Do you know this?

Do you know that life is a playground? It is for you to choose how you wish to play. And the way you choose to play is through how you feel, at any given moment, at any given time, on any given day.

Life is your playground every day. It is always for you to decide how you want to play. Do you ask yourself, "How do I wish to play today?" Do you treat your day as though it's a playground? Do you feel into the emotions that you have every given day?

We say you do. We say you very much do feel into the emotions. What we say, though, is that there are many of you not with the emotions of playing. You carry around emotions more of defeat than you do play. If your life is a playground and you are playing, let's say a game, it is that many of you step into your day, or walk through your day, with a very defeated mindset. A very defeated energetic place. And we say that it really must not have to be that way.

Yet many of you find it far easier to feel defeated than triumphant. Do you know that there is always one or the other? You are either winning or you are not. You are either triumphant or you aren't. You are either a victim or victorious.

And we say that many of you find it far easier to be defeated, perhaps even at times feeling like a victim. Just open yourselves a bit. Just allow yourself to pay attention to how you step onto your playground, your playing field. Life is your field, and you are playing on it, whether you see that or not. And it is always for you to decide on what side of the field you wish to play, the offensive side or the defensive side. We say that many play defensively.

Often times this has become your way of life, not even consciously but perhaps more subconsciously. Many of you have become quite familiar with playing defensively, not playing triumphantly. You've become quite comfortable with this, you see, and it's become quite ordinary and normal for you.

And we say it mustn't be that way. You must see yourself as the player on the field. What kind of a player are you? Are you one who sits on the bench? Are you one who sits on the sidelines?

Or are you one that is on the actual field? Think about that for a second. How you are stepping onto your day will always let you know if you are on the bench, on the sidelines, or playing on the field. You see, action is required whenever a game is played. You cannot play a game without any action steps, correct? Would you agree?

There is a need to have motion, to have movement. In addition, some would say you are on the bench waiting to play but the opportunity has not presented itself; the name has not been called. Many of you too perhaps sometimes sit on the sidelines and on the bench, waiting for just the right opportunity to come along, and we say there is never the right opportunity. There is only an opportunity.

It's very important for you to understand that. Many of you prevent yourselves from playing on the field, playing in this life, because you are waiting for the right opportunity. You are waiting for the right mate. You are waiting for the right career, the right job, the right time, the right home, the right this, the right that.

We say that there is only opportunity. How you step into that opportunity is what creates that opportunity to be right for you or not. However, one can never know without doing, you see, and therefore action is necessary. Do you agree?

So many of you wait for the right job or hold off applying for that job, waiting for the right skill set to emerge within you, waiting for the right job to come, in the right location at the right time, the right time in your life. And we say that there is no better time than now.

Do you understand what we mean? We are saying that it is very important for you and very helpful for you to understand that the game in which you're playing, that this field in life that you play upon, is always going. There is a game always playing, you see. There is always a necessary movement.

One can never win a game, a football player can never win a game, a soccer player can never win a game, a baseball player can never win a game, a tennis player can never win a game, a hockey player can never win a game without being on the field, without taking movement and action toward the game in which he is there to play. We say that you should treat life more like that, you see. Life is always presenting to you a playing field, and it is for you to decide if you wish to step onto the field.

There is no right opportunity or right timing. There is only the now. And we say the now is very important, you see, because you can only create in the now. You can only develop what is in the now. You can only build what is in the now. Taking movement, taking action, and taking steps toward anything that you wish to have requires action. It requires you to step onto the playing field, and your life is, in many ways, a playing field.

It is for you to decide what it is that you are playing, how you choose to play, how you are showing up. Are you on the bench? Are you on the sidelines or are you on the field? Stop and pause a moment to think.

Are you a player that is on the bench, waiting for the right opportunity to come along before that career opportunity can present itself? Are you waiting for the right time in your life before the right man or woman is going to show up in your life? Are you on the sidelines, waiting for that person to present that opportunity to you? Waiting for that door to knock? Or are you out there knocking on the doors? We say that it would be good to pay attention here to how you are stepping onto the playing field. At any given moment of any day, in which you are fortunate and gifted and blessed to have, it is always up to you as to how you are playing.

How are you playing? Are you going after life with zest and excitement? Do you enter your playing field of your life excited for what will be? Wanting a victory that day? Wanting to move in a direction that is closer to the finish line of your goal?

Are you going after your life with the intention of winning? And what is winning? What is winning to you? Do you see yourself as one who wins? Do you understand that you are entirely responsible for your win or your loss?

This gets some people perhaps a bit uncomfortable and they say, "I would never want to lose." And we say, "Do you really feel that?" If you look at how you step into your life, do you step into your life excited? Do you step into your day with vigor? With enthusiasm?

Do you have a mindset of winning for yourself that day? Or do you have that mindset of feeling defeated, with no excitement toward the day, not seeing how you can win at all up against a team that you can never win against.

You may call that life. What we're here to say is that you are life. And it is always for you to win it. However, do you begin your day with the intention and the mindset of winning? When we say winning in life, we mean being happy. We mean finding joy. We mean moving toward what feels good for you, you see.

This is wining, do you understand? However, do you move toward things that feel good to you? Do you move toward a direction that feels better for you? Or do you stay right where you are when things feel uneasy, when things feel uncomfortable?

Do you stay in a place that makes you feel defeated? Do you keep yourself on the sidelines watching life go by? Watching others experiencing life, having their successes, and you wonder why you aren't having any, perhaps, yourself at the moment in the areas in which you want? You must ask yourself, "Am I stepping into that area in my life, that playing field of my life, with excitement, with my desires charged, with the mindset of winning, of achieving what it is I want?" Do you?

This is for you to ask yourself. We are just here to shine a little light in this area, to let you know and understand that life is a marvelous, wondrous field of possibilities and opportunities. And the opportunities and possibilities are all over your field, all over your playground, all over your playing field.

We say that some of you perhaps sit on the sidelines and sit on the bench looking out at the playing field and watching others going after what it is that they want. We say that you could have what you wish as well.

However, there must be action toward anything that you want. There must be action toward feeling a way that you wish to feel. What we mean is that it is always important for you to move toward a place on the field that feels better. To do that, you must have action, you must move, there must be motion.

You must get off the bench and try.

We're here to say to you that for some of you, not all of you, we see that it is time to get off the bench. It is time to play and take part in this wonderful life. As you do, you'll come straight ahead with the possibilities and opportunities because they are all on the playing field and cannot be met from the bench or the sidelines.

We say to put on your jersey, tighten your laces, step off of the bench, and step onto your playing field of life, and as you place the helmet on your head, consider that your mindset of winning. Many of you feel that this game of life is difficult, too challenging. We say that it is far more challenging to stay on the sidelines. It is far more challenging to keep yourself on the bench. As you stay on the sidelines and you stay on the bench, you keep yourself from all possibilities and all opportunities. When you begin to move with them, you will find those that feel like the right opportunity. However, they will never be found on the sidelines or on the bench.

We say move. Try. Play. Get out there. Take part in this glorious game called life and know that you are a very important player, for yourself and for those that are around you who are playing with you.

We wish simply to give you something to think about. Think about your life as a playing field, think about where you are positioning yourself on that playing field or if in fact you are on that playing field at all. Are you watching from a distance? Watching life go by? Or are you interacting with it, taking part of it, playing in it. That is something only you can answer. We merely come forward to ask you the question. We say that there is no wrong answer; there is only the answer that is in this moment. However, you can change at any given moment how you position yourself on that playing field.

That is always in your control. Isn't it wonderful to know that you can decide where you position yourself on your playing field in life? The only thing that has kept you in that position has been yourself, and the only one who can bring you there is also yourself.

You see, you are a very important player on your field of life. What kind of player are you? That is for you to answer. If you are recognizing that you have not been quite the player that you should have been, know and understand that just by becoming aware of that, you can change that entirely.

That too is your power. We wish you all to be winners in your life. We wish you all to play and to enjoy the life in which you are in, for it is meant to be enjoyed. However, to enjoy it, you must know and understand the way you step in to play. Sometimes there needs to be a flashlight placed among each of you so you can see if your jersey is on at all, to always know and understand that you can always place the jersey on you if you realize it has not been on. This too is in your power.

We look forward to seeing all the ways in which you now step into your playing field and enjoy the way you are playing in it. It is so.

We thank you for this time and this opportunity to be with you in this way. It gives us much happiness to come forward, to give you once again a little more to put your attention toward, to ask yourself the questions that help you become more aware of as to how you are stepping into the beautiful life that you have been gifted to live.

It is so. Until next time, there is great love for you here.

Edgar

About the author

Monica Teurlings is an evidential medium, channel, teacher, speaker and author. She is married to her husband Joe and has two grown children, Kyle and Cole. She lives in Southern California with her husband and her golden retriever rescue, Zoey.

Visit her upcoming events page online for a list of workshops she teaches, live mediumship demonstrations and small group events she does both online and in an area near you.

If you would like a personal reading with Monica, visit her website, where you can book a session with her either online on zoom, in person or over the phone.

If you are interested in hosting a small group reading either in person or over Zoom or would like to hire Monica for an event, please reach out to her directly at the number below.

Follow her on social media:
Facebook: @MonicaTeurlingsPM
Instagram: @MonicaTeurlingsMedium
Twitter: @mediummonica
Visit her website at www.monicateurlings.com

Monica's first book with Edgar titled: "Destination Self: Navigated for You with Love from My Spirit Guides" is available on Amazon, Barnes & Noble and through her book page on her website.

Contact Monica Teurlings:
Email: info@monicateurlings.com
Phone: 949-377-1221 (w)

Printed in the United States
By Bookmasters